CAVEMEN CAN'T MARKET

ATTRACTING, CONVERSING, AND CREATING LOYAL CUSTOMERS WITH WOO MARKETING™

by

Jonathan Peters, Ph.D.

CAVEMEN CAN'T MARKET

ATTRACTING, CONVERSING, AND CREATING LOYAL CUSTOMERS WITH WOO MARKETING™

by

Jonathan Peters, Ph.D.

Circumference Press

Cavemen Can't Market: Attracting, Conversing, and Creating Loyal Customers with WOO Marketing™

Cover art by Kimb Manson Graphic Design
www.senjula.com

ISBN: 978-

Printed in the United States of America

CONTENTS

ONCE UPON A TIME...

A CAVEMAN SAW A BEAUTIFUL WOMAN WALKING PAST.

HE PICKED UP HIS CLUB, HIT HER OVER THE HEAD, AND DRAGGED HER INTO HIS CAVE.

AND SHE BECAME HIS WIFE.

AND IT BECAME KNOWN AS MARKETING.

THE PROBLEM WAS...

WOMEN DON'T LIKE BEING HIT OVER THE HEAD.

THEY'D RATHER BE WOOED.

THEY BANDED TOGETHER TO PUT THE CAVEMAN OUT OF BUSINESS.

NOW THEY ONLY LISTENED TO SUITORS WHO ATTRACTED THEM, CONVERSED WITH THEM, AND DE-VELOPED A RELATIONSHIP WITH THEM.

AND THE COURTSHIP ERA BEGAN...

1

THE BEGINNING

Maybe it's in our DNA. Maybe it's just that it's always been done this way. But for some reason, marketing continues to look and feel like a Caveman is doing it.

Visualize a Caveman lounging on his stone, club at his side, not much going on in his head.

Then a beautiful woman wanders past.

The Caveman tries to whistle, but that skill hasn't been developed yet. So he grunts.

She hears him, turns, looks him over, and walks quickly away.

His response? He picks up his club, rushes up behind her, clubs her over the head, drags her back to his cave. And she becomes his wife.

And marketers are still using techniques like this to get customers.

Well, they aren't physically hitting customers over the head. Just metaphorically.

They have their USPs, elevator pitches, brands, or whatever collateral they're smashing over people's heads.

And they swing that message and collateral until the prospect collapses under the force of their blows.

Ad after ad after ad interrupts people's lives. They can't enjoy their favorite show or listen to more than a couple of songs without a club crashing down on their heads. They can't drive down the street without being broadsided by a billboard. Even their mailbox is filled with unnecessary bulk. And what about dinner and the ringing phone?, Or spam? Everywhere prospects turn, they see a club swinging toward their heads.

In the old days it worked.
Why? Because marketers had money to keep the clubs swinging. And prospects had soft heads. Eventually, a prospect would collapse under the pressure, and the marketers would drag the now limp customer into their caves.

But she wasn't happy with the situation.

But where else would she go? In his cave she had fire, food, and protection. Outside the cave, there were dangers and other Cavemen swinging clubs.

Fortunately for her, things changed for the Caveman. Suddenly prospects put up a resistance. Getting customers wasn't as simple as swinging a club. And this confused him.

Prospects began building armor to defend against the harangues of marketers. They created helmets, shields, and even body armor.

So marketers had to get sneakier. Interruption marketing made sure prospects couldn't eat a meal without the phone ringing. (Back then, they had to answer the phone because there was no caller ID.) Letters looked like they were from a friend but were actually pitch pieces. Even ads in newspapers looked like articles.

Later, emails looked like honest calls for help from poor people in Nigeria. Internet searches were hijacked by meta tags. And the ads increased in intensity and prevalence.

Marketers hit harder, longer, and louder, making unbearable dents, until the noise became so loud it was easier for prospects to give in than resist.

But when they did give in, the customers weren't happy. They felt duped, manipulated, and taken for granted.

So prospects developed a better strategy; instead of resisting the marketers, they gathered where the marketers weren't. They built their own communities, forts of a sort, that kept the marketers away.

> Things work
> until they don't.

Swinging clubs was no longer effective. Either prospects were no longer standing where the Cavemen were swinging, or the clubs hit against walls, jarring the hands of the marketers.

Confused, the marketers kept swinging, because that's what they'd always done. They swung harder and faster. They teamed up with others to hit sections of the fort's walls. Others began swinging at other Cavemen to keep the battle going.

But eventually the absurdity of it all left them pooped and scratching their heads. They looked at the thick walls in front of them and wondered why no one invited them to the new era.

Grunting and rutting, the Cavemen circled the new communities, trying to find a way in. They noticed a new kind of man who easily slipped into the forts. He only had to smile, sing, engage, entertain, and (dare I say) seduce, and the doors opened for him.

What just happened? How is it that this man in all his finery was able to do what the Cavemen couldn't? He didn't have a club. He didn't use force. And he did silly things like sing and recite poetry to be able to access the prospects.

He also didn't think of prospects as prospects, but as Intendeds. He understood that they needed to be courted and WOOed instead of manhandled. He understood that old marketing methods EWed his Intendeds, and that it was his responsibility to be attractive to Intendeds, and engage them in conversation. When this happened, they'd begin a relationship with him.

And so the Suitor replaced the Caveman. Prospects appreciated his methods. They welcomed him into their community. And they recommended him to others.

Why? Because prospects love to be courted and hate to be hit on the head. Those marketers that understood this fundamental point got access, while Cavemen were re-buffed. Prospects resisted the club but opened themselves up to courtship.

As marketing changed, the Caveman became not only irrelevant, but also reviled. Meanwhile, the Suitor was not only appreciated, but embraced.

And thus began WOO marketing.

Glossary

Suitor: The marketing person who understands this is a new era in marketing, that marketers are no longer in charge of the message nor the spreading of the message, and that now we must WOO prospects. While the Suitor is a young man in storybooks, in the marketing world he can be a man or a woman. This is not a PC analogy.

Cavemen: Marketers who use outdated marketing methods. And while it is non-PC to say "Caveman" instead of "Caveperson," let's face it, most of the ancient marketers were men.

Intendeds: Prospects. They are not yet customers, but we'd like them to be. Of course, in the real world, many of our Intendeds may be men, but in the storybooks, the Intended is a damsel who has many Suitors to choose from. (What are we teaching children?)

WOO: The marketing techniques used by Suitors to develop a relationship with Intendeds.

EW: Marketing methods used by Cavemen that repel Intendeds.

The Courtship Era: The relationship between companies and prospects changed with the rise of social media. In the Courtship Era, Intendeds are in charge. Marketers must interact with them where they are and in ways that they appreciate.

WARNING!

The WOO approach is based on an analogy. It's an old story. And like all old stories, this one is **NOT** politically correct.

It's boy falls in love with girl. He seeks to attract the girl; she resists the boy; he continues to charm her until she yields to his WOOing; and finally, finally, she gives him the desired kiss.

Of course he wants more than a kiss, so he continues WOOing, and she continues to run him through trials and tribulations until eventually she agrees to marry him.

This book is about this story. It is a tongue-in-cheek analogy for the new landscape of marketing.

If you don't have a sense of humor, or are so literal as to think I mean that all marketers are men and all prospects are women, and that I'm somehow proselytizing an alternative lifestyle of one man and one woman, or are distracted by whatever hang up you might have for the old story of boy loves girl, **please quit reading**. You'll be too fixated on the symbolism to understand the message.

Set down this book. Maybe return it for a refund. Burn it if it makes you feel better.

You may already be happily or unhappily married. You may be a woman who pursues men, or a woman who has no use for men. Maybe you are a man who has no use for woman or some other contrary combination.

I am not suggesting in these pages that you must be a man in pursuit of a woman to successfully market. And I acknowledge that you may be uncomfortable with the idea that you should be pursuing multiple Intendeds.

This book is an analogy and is not meant to threaten the sanctity of marriage, especially your marriage.

This is a story about marketing. It uses an analogy to communicate marketing challenges, methods, and perspectives. It is a "for-instance," a "it's-kinda-like." And within the analogy there are insights. But it's not meant to be taken literally, nor even seriously.

Now that I have that off my chest, let's proceed...

Jonathan Peters, Ph.D.

How Did We Get Here?

A Short History of Marketing from Caveman days to the Courtship Era

THE LITTLE HOUSE ON THE PRAIRIE

Are you old enough to remember the books or the television show *Little House on the Prairie*?

Me neither.

But back when there were little houses on the prairies, things were different, especially when it came to hooking up with a spouse.

A young man had only a few options, mostly the neighbors' daughters. There weren't many of them (neighbors I mean). And his choices weren't usually definitions of beauty.

And if he wasn't careful, his family tree would be without limbs.

There was a certain desperateness in his pursuit. With limited "customers," and a few competitors that included his brothers, he had to differentiate himself, and look attractive to a woman's father, for it was his responsibility to demonstrate his ability to live up to the father's expectations before courting a young woman.

But in the end, if he didn't mess up too badly, he had little competition, especially after he put his brothers in their places. Sure he might not get the most beautiful woman in the community, but he would get someone. After all, fathers needed to get rid of their daughters, and women couldn't survive on their own back then.

So the young woman needed a man to own the farm, work the farm, and fix things. He needed a wife to crank out children to help work the farm, raise those children, prepare meals, and tend the house.

Imagine a customer needing your product at that level. What if their very survival depended on acquiring your product? It wouldn't be about wanting your product, or desiring it, but needing it to survive.

That's what it was like in the Little House on the Prairie days. They bought things that they needed, and little else. Even the wealthiest only had a few changes of clothes. Why would you need more than one dress or one collared shirt? Yes, you might want more than two work outfits, but you only really needed one coat and one pair of shoes. Even if you had extra clothes, where would you store them? Without closets in your small bedroom, too many clothes would be a problem.

So marketing back then was as simple as finding a need, and solving it. Yes, there were manufacturing, distribution, and brand awareness issues, but for the most part, you would provide something they needed, and they'd buy it on their next trip to town.

From a marketing perspective, it also didn't matter if a customer needed a variation of a staple product. If they were too big, too skinny, too tall, or too short, they had to adjust. If they needed or wanted something that the majority of their neighbors didn't need, they'd have to do without.

Sears and Roebuck recognized this problem and offered tons of products in their catalogs. But even then, choices and sizes were limited.

And delivery was also slow on the Prairie. If you needed something today or this week, you were in trouble. You either turned to your local store on your next trip to town or waited for the mail to take your order to Sears and Roebuck, and they'd eventually coordinate with the trains to get it to you.

On the Prairie, marketing was about being nearby. You had the store, and they came to you. You delivered a catalog and they bought from it.

Once there were needs, now we have wants.

All you needed to do was supply what was generally needed to your local market, and you would make money.

This means there wasn't such a thing as niche marketing. You needed broad appeal to afford to bring a product across the Prairie to a small community. It was one-size-fits-all retail.

The shopkeeper only had so much shelf space, and he had common needs and interests to cover. There needs like food for all three meals, house supplies, and personal products (though these were few back then). Then there were the "luxury" and impulse items such as a piece of candy or tube of lipstick.

Shopkeepers couldn't afford to vary beyond those things that everyone needed to survive. True, if someone wanted something specific, there was a catalog somewhere, but for the most part, people purchased what the shopkeeper provided, and the shopkeeper restricted his provisions to items the majority of his customers needed because he didn't have room to store inventory.

Plus, customers didn't come around often.

Once a week, or even once a month, the family would pile into the wagon and ride into town where they'd do all their shopping in one trip.

Not only were their options limited to what the store owner put before them, the concept of brand was limited. Certain brands became staples in the barn and in the kitchen, but only because the Shopkeeper was able to obtain those brands. The Shopkeeper didn't have enough room, nor inclination to risk the inventory, to have more than one brand of oats, sugar, or petroleum jelly. And while he might take the risk to offer candy or lipstick, he could only offer one brand.

So any Caveman could market back then. All you had to do was get to the village, incentivize the shopkeeper to carry your product, convince people they needed your product, and you were in.

It was like being the last man on the planet.

AND THE CAVEMAN REIGNED

Customers were gullible on the Prairie. With so few brands and marketing messages, they hadn't built up a resistance to a good delivery. Traveling salesmen were not only able to sell snake oil, longevity, or salvation, people honestly thought they needed these things.

Think of a sheltered damsel. She's worked on her father's farm her whole life. And every once in a while she would see a boy when she was in town, but she never actually talked to one. She didn't have any references beyond what her parents and siblings told her about boys and marriage. There may have been books available on the subject, but she didn't have television programs, or the Internet.

So when a Dandy came into town from Back East, he could beguile the gullible creature, sweep her off her feet, and ultimately break her heart.

And that's what marketing was like back then. A Caveman could convince anyone to buy anything. He only had to walk out to their farm, strike up a conversation in the village, or grandstand at the carnival.

The Caveman would prey on fears and desires, suggest a need, appeal to different motivators, use certain persuasion techniques, grab up people's money, and get the hell out of town before people figured out they had been duped.

On the Prairie, a good marketer needed only to have a lack of conscience and an elevated greed to get people to buy his product. Competition was minimal and prospects were gullible. Even a Caveman could market.

Interruption Marketing is Born

When the traveling salesman stopped by the farm, the farmer set down his tools and listened to the presentation, or the wife stopped toiling long enough to look at the pictures in his catalog. But these small interactions were actually more like distractions than interruptions. The folks on the Prairie welcomed the salesman and his wares.

Things changed with the radio era. Entertainment came into the house. Families gathered around the radio to hear news, variety shows, and serial stories.

Competition was still limited on this new medium. Only those who could afford to get ads on the radio, or in the magazines and newspapers were able to market.

As families gathered around their radios for their favorite programs, Cavemen found a way to swing their clubs. People wanted to hear their shows, so the Cavemen inserted themselves into the shows. They rudely interrupted the family experience with commercial breaks.

And what was a listener to do? If they turned off the radio, they wouldn't know when the show was back on. They couldn't switch channels because they might miss something when dialing back. And dialing between the channels was a complicated process.

So with the rise of radio, the Caveman invented a marketing strategy that would frustrate customers for a very long time. Consumers wanted to listen to their program, and Cavemen rudely interrupted.

But despite all the frustration, what could a person do? Listeners, and later, viewers, simply had to put up with rude interruption.

And Cavemen hadn't even discovered the telephone yet.

It Didn't Change Much During the Television Era

L ittle changed with the arrival of the television. It was, after all, essentially a visual radio. Yes, the tactics changed a bit, but the Cavemen still reigned.

You're probably not old enough to remember a time when there were only three commercial television stations plus one public station. The three networks' main concern was how to have as broad an appeal as possible to beat out their competitors. They feared that their viewers would stray toward a competitor, but let's be honest, what else were people going to do in the evening besides watch television. It was easier than, say, reading a book.

With more viewers and more popular programs, the three stations could charge more for ads. It was a tough balance, of course, between the number of ads shown and the quality of the program. After all, their customers were not the people watching the shows, but the advertisers who were buying access to the viewers. If viewers became too frustrated with all the ads, they'd leave, and then advertisers would leave as well. So it was about keeping viewers long enough to sell them to advertisers.

You also may not remember that there was a time when most Americans were in one place on Thursday evenings: their couches. For years, NBC dominated the Thursday evening time slot, and anyone who was anyone watched the same "must see TV" programs week after week.

I'm sure some people were watching the other networks, or maybe not even watching television at all, but these people were left out of conversations rehashing *Cheers, The Cosbys, Friends,* or *Seinfield* the next day.

With so many people in one spot watching one television program at the same time, advertisers salivated at the opportunity to give a single message to so many people.

All they needed was a big enough club to swing the high price, and they could be confident that large numbers of people would hear their message. And the more money they had, the more times they could run their ad, and the more likely they were to land a blow.

Of course the message had to be broad enough to appeal to the whole viewing audience. So to get the biggest bang for their battering rams, marketers spoke at as many people as possible. If a viewer didn't line up with their defined demographics, companies simply ignored them.

Now that we were watching television, we were exposed to so many more items we could buy and experiences we could have. We began to define ourselves by what we owned.

Suddenly it wasn't about satisfying survival needs, but acquiring things so we could live the lives we saw on television. We are being socialized to be consumers.

No longer did we go to the store to learn about products, we were introduced to them in our own homes. We weren't limited by a store's inventory, but had access to all that was available.

And since the only way we could acquire what we wanted was to travel to the store to buy, stores were forced to get bigger, to carry the items that commercials had created a demand for.

And so superstores were created to shelve all those items, competing brands, and stuff we didn't know we needed.

Sure consumers had more choices, but they also had fewer choices. Markets were broad, products appealed to as many people as possible, and few alternatives were available beyond what the majority wanted.

> Commercials create a desire for items we would not otherwise have desired.

Niche products were a luxury. And small upstarts didn't have the money to reach people who would be interested in their offering.

Consumers were socialized to identify with brands. You were a Coke or a Pepsi person. You drove a GM or a Ford. You drank Miller or Bud. And you wanted your stores to carry these items.

And now that consumers knew what brands they wanted before getting to the store, staff didn't need to help or educate customers. Service began disappearing in the big stores. Without a proprietor who cared about his or her customers, employees didn't bother to cultivate a relationship that might exist beyond making the sale.

Furthermore, now that all these new products were being hammered over our heads, our desire for more stuff increased faster than our incomes. To get what we wanted, we needed things to be cheap.

When you're competing on price and quantity, you have to cut something. Service was the least tangible aspect of business, so it needed to go.

Also, with the big stores, there was a need for more employees. The proprietor was far removed from the customers, and low wage employees became the face of the business. These employees were not being compensated for going beyond the basics; therefore, they had little motivation to serve customers.

You could gripe all you wanted, but if you wanted the lowest price possible, you had to put up with the lack of service.

After all, it wasn't really about customers, but about what and how much they bought. In a mass market world, customers are treated as units and not individuals. People were placed in broad demographics. We became a group, a stereotype, and there wasn't room for singularity.

So we now pump our own gas, bag our own groceries, and talk to a computer or someone in another country when we have a problem.

Because no Caveman wants to talk with a customer.

And Then Came the World Wide Web

Unless you lost money during the Dotcom Boom and Bust, you may not remember what an amazing time Web 1.0 was.

All you had to do was have a website and you were in business. The chess club geek could compete with the football captain. Or, to stay with our metaphor, the skinny intellectual could compete with the big, strong jock. The little guy didn't need a big budget, huge staff, or access to large media outlets. A simple website was enough.

Big companies took little notice that the scrawny were cutting in on their territory. They were so out of touch with their customers that they didn't notice the few that left to hang out with dotcomers. In their big offices, the big boys felt protected from this new thing called the World Wide Web.

After all, the big boys had financial and positional power. Who could take over their shelf space? If an upstart started encroaching, the big boys had enough money to buy them before they got too big. They had the distribution and the knowledge to keep others away from customers.

Traditional media also felt secure during these days because they had monopolies on information. Television and newspapers edited information for us; they told us what was important.

But entrepreneurs understood the potential of the Web. They could play a different game. They could get to where the big companies weren't. They could deliver messages directly to customers instead of buying expensive and intrusive ads. When people were ready to buy, they didn't have to go to the store; they could buy right now in their own living rooms.

Sure these startups didn't have the discipline of larger companies, but they did have ideas, energy, and excitement.

Customers were thrilled that products were available all the time. Whatever they wanted, whenever they wanted it. All was a click and a credit card away.

And they didn't need to go to a store. They didn't need to interact with a person. In fact, they didn't even need to know the name of the company they were buying from, as long as they trusted the buying process.

The upstarts didn't have to touch or talk to their customers. Automation reigned as companies eliminated interaction with their customers.

And if you had a complaint, what would you do? Without someone to talk to at the store, who would listen? There might be a phone number or an email address, but really, who was listening?

With the costs of doing business so low, the potential for profits was immense. Those were exciting days during the boom. The stock market wouldn't slow down. Irrational exuberance reigned. Of course it would end, but what was driving the boom was a new view of how people would interact.

It was like changing from having to ask the father's permission for his daughter, to having thousands of options throughout the world, and with no fathers to negotiate with.

And this is where a lot of marketing failed in those years, and why, ultimately, the boom busted. With so many new options and opportunities, mar-

> *Things work until they don't. And when they don't, get rid of them.*

keters didn't adjust. They tried to modify Caveman tactics to the new medium, and it didn't work.

Email blasts became spam. Pop-up ads interrupted a search. Search engine manipulation frustrated searchers. Websites teased, but didn't deliver.

While customers were now in charge of their own searches, they began to feel even more disconnected from their sellers. They were simply buying on price.

Of course, some companies got it. Amazon didn't stop at just selling books at a discount; they created an experience. They reached out to customers, made them feel like they were being listened to. They WOOed customers away from the bookstores, and changed the buying experience. And that is why Amazon survived where so many dotcom companies failed. They focused on the customer.

With the rise of the World Wide Web, Cavemen still reigned, but with the dotcom bust, their usefulness came into question. People began to perceive a different way, one where they could be in charge, where marketers would have to come to them, bend a knee, and ask for their permission.

WEB 2.0 ENDED
THE CAVEMAN ERA

And then came social media, and what has been called Web 2.0. Suddenly, consumers were in charge. Cavemen could no longer lurk in the HTML shadows. Even large companies were exposed as shells of power. And traditional media quickly lost its footing in relevancy.

People watched programs when they wanted to watch them. They skipped over commercials. They created their own communities away from the domain of marketers. And they began having their own unmonitored conversations with others.

Social media allowed customers to find people who were similar to them, who had similar values, interests, and priorities (VIPs). They discovered that they didn't have to be like an entire demographic; instead, they could hang out with people just like them. Better yet, they didn't have to buy what everyone else was buying. They could find products just for them. They could be individuals instead of a group.

And that's when consumers realized their power. They had a voice. People and companies could listen to them on different platforms, from blogs to social media postings. If they didn't like something, they could spread the word faster than a company could run an ad campaign.

For instance, have you heard that United Airlines breaks guitars?

According to musician Dave Carroll, United Airlines baggage handlers threw his guitar on the tarmac. When he got to Omaha, Nebraska, he discovered that his guitar's neck was broken. When he filed a claim, United told him that he was not eligible for compensation because he didn't file the claim within 24 hours of the incident.

Carroll didn't give up. He continued to seek compensation for the next nine months. Then he got so frustrated he decided to write a song and produce a music video about United breaking his guitar and the lousy customer service he received.

When the first music video went up on YouTube, it had over 150,000 views within the first day. Three days later, over half a million people had seen the video. And seven months later, more than 10 million had viewed the video.

The week following the video's release, it was the number one song on iTunes.

United contacted Carroll shortly after the video was put up. They wanted to apologize for the way he and his guitar were treated, and they offered to give $3,000 to the Thelonious Monk Institute of Jazz as a goodwill gesture.

But the gesture didn't matter. Four days after the video was posted, United's stock prices dropped 10%, costing stockholders $180 million in the value of their stock. Of course, many things could have caused the stock prices to drop, but if I had United stocks at the time, I know I would have dumped my stock when I realized the video was going viral.

The guitar that was broken was a Taylor. And since it's featured in the video, Taylor Guitars immediately gave Carroll two guitars, and props for his second music video.

Why did Taylor Guitars do this? Because they saw the opportunity for free advertising. Millions of people were about to see their guitars featured in the video. And it was in their best interest to support the production of the next two videos.

And United? Well their donation didn't get much press. In fact, most of the people telling others about the video weren't aware of the gesture. What they were aware of was how United breaks guitars, and how they responded to Carroll.

A customer could not have had this much impact before social media. They could complain, tell their friends, maybe even organize a boycott, but they wouldn't have this kind of impact.

> *Word of mouth has become WORLD of mouth*

And now I'm telling you about the video. So the message is still spreading years later.

With social media, people can tell their experiences and hear about other's experiences. They can ask about a company, get advice, and generally discuss their interests and concerns.

Companies are mostly outside the conversation. The Cavemen can swing their clubs all they want, but no one is there to receive their blows. In fact, they are talking to each other about those silly Cavemen swinging clubs. And if someone is hit or hurt, everyone will run to their defense, and punish the Cavemen.

Back on the Prairie, consumers were dependent on Cavemen for survival. But in the new world, consumers realized that they aren't dependent after all.

Now that they didn't need Cavemen for survival, customers wanted a relationship. They wanted to identify with products and companies. They didn't want to be advertised to, they wanted to be WOOed.

The key in the Social Media Era is creating a relationship with customers. One can't simply swing a club at a prospect because she would report it to her friends, and they would band together to punish the brute. A Caveman can't entice with a message because prospects get advice from their own communities. And it is no longer a one-size-fits-all world; prospects began to not only realize their own identities, interests, and priorities, they also began to demand that companies work with them.

The relationship between marketer and consumer forever changed with the advent of social media. Now the consumer is in charge, and successful marketers WOO them. Meanwhile, the Caveman has become irrelevant.

WHAT'S LOVE GOT TO DO WITH IT?

While we're talking about relationships, and the new era, let's also look at the history of love...

The concept of love in a relationship is a relatively recent occurrence. It wasn't that long ago that a man wanted someone to tend his house and raise his children. He would bargain with a father. They would haggle over price. The daughter had very little influence in the negotiation.

Falling in love was not part of the contract. He promised to provide; she promised to provide.

The emergence of chivalry during the Middle Ages introduced the radical concept of love. But even then, you didn't love your spouse; you loved your suitor or mistress.

So what does this mean for us? Buying and selling, bargaining and cajoling, and conquering and contracting clients are methods used by Cavemen. They no longer work, just as the old way of negotiating for a mate no longer works. In the new era, we need to shift to courtship.

Courtship is a process of WOOing. The young man must first find ways to attract her. Can you strum a mandolin? Recite poetry? Buy trinkets?

In the old days, the Caveman took what he wanted, or negotiated for what he could not freely take. In other words, he could advertise on a program whether the viewer wanted him to or not. He could mail or email someone whether or not they wanted to receive his correspondence.

In the Courtship Era, prospects must change from being prospects to being Intendeds. Once we understand that we can't simply pound our messages, that they must be WOOed, we will change our attitudes towards prospects, and market differently.

In the Courtship Era, marketers must view themselves as Suitors. As such, they must stand out in the crowd, and provide that which is attractive to a specific client.

The techniques and tools for WOOing are endless thanks to social media and other platforms. And the more creative we are, the more our customers will take notice.

As a Suitor, don't think of Intendeds as people who must be conquered and corralled, but as someone who needs to be courted. First, be attractive to them; then engage them in conversation. Find out what is important to them. What their values, interests, and priorities are. What issues you can solve. And how you can be of service.

And then invite them, through a series of small commitments, to be in a relationship with you. Don't ask for too much too soon; simply draw them closer and closer.

And if you do things well, you will have a loyal and committed customer. At the end of the day, isn't that what we want? Not just a series of quick purchases, but a committed and loyal customer base who not only purchase from us, but who also tells others about how wonderful it is to have a relationship with us.

This is the Way of WOO.

Jonathan Peters, Ph.D.

Prepare To WOO

Before we can WOO them, we have to be ready for them.

Are You Where They Are?

In the old days, consumers came to companies. They came to our stores and websites. They watched our programs and read our publications.

In the new era, the Courtship Era, we must go to them, interact with them where they are, and sell them what they want, when they want it.

Think back ten years... to when you were in middle school.

Do you remember what the cafeteria looked like back then? All the boys sat on one side of the cafeteria, and all the girls sat on the other side.

How silly, right? With all those new hormones haunting the blood stream, the boys ached to talk with the girls, and I'm sure the girls swooned to have a boy select them for conversation. And yet we sat on separate sides of the cafeteria, glancing at each other, but never closing the divide between boys and girls.

Have you noticed we still do that today?

I spend a lot of time in bars, not because I have a problem... yet. But because I don't want to eat alone. The lonely table doesn't work for me, so I sit at the bar because that is where the people are, and where conversations are meant to happen.

I've noticed that we still sit with the boys on one side and girls on the other. The men sit shoulder-to-shoulder at the bar, while behind them group the women at tall tables and booths.

Now, can we assume that some of the men came to the bar to talk with ladies? And that some of the ladies came to the bar to talk with men?

And yet the men sit with their backs to the ladies. And the ladies gather in intimidating groups, glancing at the men, maybe commenting on the men, but always keeping their distance, and the space between the two groups clear.

Isn't that how we are with our marketing? Even if we're in the same room as our Intendeds, we're still not in a position to converse with them.

We make sure our presence is noticed, but we keep a distance between us. Our logo is tacked in the lower right corner of the ad. We're blasting their email accounts. Bragging on our timelines. But we're not actually talking with our Intendeds.

It's like a Suitor getting all dressed up to meet ladies at the local establishment. He saunters past the tables and plops at the bar. He orders his beer, and looks around. Behind him a gaggle of Intendeds huddle around a table. They may want what he's selling, but they aren't approaching him. They may look his way, size him up, comment to their friends, but they don't approach him.

Most marketers are content to sit at the bar and stare back at their prospects. They let their designs, messages, and SWAG speak for them. They are fine with their ad being in the sight-line of their Intendeds. They wait, and hope to get noticed. They are paying for impressions.

And they go home alone wondering why they failed.

Of course Intendeds don't make it easier for them.

In the Caveman days, he could walk into a bar, grab the one he wanted, and leave. Now, poor Suitors must do all the hard work.

But isn't it true that we are more comfortable sitting at the bar with our buddies than crossing the divide to engage our Intendeds? In fact, the more desirous our Intendeds

The strong, silent type will be alone. She may find him attractive, but will ultimately choose the one who talks to her.

are, the more we cower away from them. Why do we avoid the people who should be our clients and customers? Why do we continue to build walls and moats between our group and the group we're trying to reach?

Because we are scared. And because we were socialized to be this way.

Follow me back to middle school (I hope I'm not bringing up too many stuttering memories).

Remember that boy who first crossed the fjord between the girls' side of the cafeteria and the boys' side? All the boys admired him, looked up to him, and told others how they could never do what he did.

It took tremendous guts, daring, and the risk of ridicule to leave the safety of the social group for the potential minefield of the girls' side. What if the girls laughed at him? What if they ignored him? What if they out right rejected him? How could he ever cross back to the boys' side of the cafeteria? Upon his return, the boys would also reject and ridicule him, and he'd have no one to eat lunch with.

This creates what we call approach anxiety. It is easier to peacock on the bar stool than to risk approaching an Intended and being rejected not only by her, but also in front of her friends and our friends.

As any good Suitor knows, rewards do go to those who make the effort to approach Intendeds, engage them in conversation, and win them over. And any good Suitor knows how heavy the phone can be, how nerve-wracking a sales call can be, and how scary it is to ask for the sale. A good Suitor also knows that the sooner he gets off his butt and approaches an Intended, the more quickly he'll succeed.

The good news is we have spaces where it is relatively easy to approach Intendeds. After all, they are conversing, asking for advice, pinning their interests, and sharing with others. On social media platforms we can join them without crossing a great divide, with relatively little risk of being mocked when we stumble and stutter.

But Cavemen act badly in these spaces. They barge into the conversation, bragging about their products and services, trying tricks to lure Intendeds, and ultimately scaring away those who might otherwise be interested in them.

For WOO to work, we must do more than look good at the bar; we need to approach the Intendeds' table and engage them in conversation. With social media, we have the opening lines, but even these need to be finessed. Lines may break the barrier, but to truly engage we need wit and the ability to talk with them, to ask the right questions, and to provide the answers.

We need to get off our stools, cross the cafeteria, and engage them in conversation.

EXERCISE: Brainstorm about where your Intendeds hang out. Research the social media platforms they hang out in, and list them here:

_____

_____

_____

_____

Choose a post from an Intended on each platform and create an opening line response for that post here:

_____

_____

_____

_____

_____

_____

_____

_____

_____

Do They
Notice You?

It is estimated that each of us is exposed to 3,000 marketing messages a day. How many of those messages are you aware of?

Quick, name three television ads you saw in the last 24 hours? What about billboards? What were the offerings in the vending machine you passed?

In the old days, it was easier to get the Intendeds' attention. There were only so many people in the village. An Intended had few options. A Suitor only had to stand slightly taller, be slightly more muscular, maybe have slightly more coins in his pocket.

But those days are gone. Our Intendeds now have too many options. Thousands of messages vie for their attention every day. Worse, they aren't even looking in our direction.

So how does a Suitor get noticed?

By not being ordinary.

The next time you are in an airport, a mall, or some other space where numbers of strangers pass each other, be aware of how many people you actually notice.

The strikingly attractive? Certainly.

Those with a specific sense of fashion? Yes.

The oddly shaped? Oh yeah; sometimes they even distract us from the truly beautiful.

The flailing, screaming child? Definitely (Why do they keep making them?)

But now be aware of those whom you don't notice.

Is it true that there are more people you are not noticing than those who attract your eye and attention?

In a crowd, there will be only a few beautiful people, a few odd ones, a couple of truly ugly ones, and fortunately a limited number of brats. So why don't we notice all of the others?

Because we have filters. And this is a good thing. Our brain filters out the usual and the ordinary, so that we can focus on the attractive, the unpleasant, and maybe even the dangerous.

What does this mean for the Suitor?

If your Intendeds' brains are wired to filter out the usual and the ordinary, will they notice you?

The problem is we are also wired to be normal. We criticize and ostracize those who do not conform with the herd. And while rewards do go to those who are different from everyone else, and while we might wish to be them, few people ever strive to be different than their peers.

This was especially true when we were young. We had to wear certain clothes, have certain hairstyles, speak a certain way, and even rebel in a similar manner. For instance, have you noticed that even those rebelling against norms end up looking like each other? Why is a Mohawk always down the middle of the head? If you truly wanted to be different, why not a side Mohawk or one that goes from ear to ear?

Let's go back to middle school. We've already established that the boy crossing over to the girl's side was praised and rewarded, but what happened when the girl crossed from her side of the cafeteria to the boy's side?

They called her a slut.

There was tremendous peer pressure to keep her on her side of the cafeteria. The other girls did not want her changing the balance of the market. They didn't want to be compelled to cross the room to get their own boyfriend. Worse, they were afraid the boys would be looking at her instead of them.

> *The peacock preens. There is nothing ordinary about him. He is noticed, and he gets the hen.*

So they called her a slut.

Similarly, there are market pressures to keep us looking and feeling like everyone else in our sector. If you stand out, you will get criticism. Peer pressure will push you back toward the norm.

And yet, when we are noticed, when we are attractive to our Intendeds, we will be rewarded by them.

This is where thinking outside the lines, thinking differently, being different, standing out, and whatever other cliches we might throw around, come in. When we are normal, we fade into the background; when we stand out, whether because we are attractive or because we are oddly shaped, people take notice.

The key is to find a way to be noticed in a way that hasn't been done before. Remember the Mohawks that look the same? Simply taking one good idea and making it yours is not enough. You need to take that extra step, to become what no one else has been in your niche.

Then you'll be noticed.

To be anything else will result in being a cliché or ordinary. And neither is noticed. Any attempts at being a Suitor will be forestalled. You'll be relegated to standing along the wall, wishing someone would ask you to dance.

Yes, those who get noticed get criticized. But if you're focused on your Intended, and understand what attracts her, what she wants, you will not be criticized by the one who matters—your Intended.

All other criticism is just jealousy from competitors and peers pressuring to keep you within the box. Consider the source.

So focus on your Intended, and damn all other critics.

EXERCISE: Brainstorm wild ways you can stand out. Think sideways Mohawks. For now, don't worry about frightening them with your crazy hair—think about being noticed. Later, you can make sure that your plumes are actually attractive to her. This is an exercise in outside-the-box thinking.

_____

_____

_____

_____

_____

_____

_____

_____

_____

_____

_____

_____

_____

_____

_____

_____

_____

_____

_____

_____

_____

First Impressions Matter

Being noticed isn't enough. She's got to like what she sees...

...within the first 4 seconds.

That is how quickly we judge whether or not someone is desirable or dangerous. Whether we'll buy or pass.

And whatever conclusions we reach in those few seconds will stay with us for as long as we are in a relationship with the person, or, for that matter, an organization.

For instance, let's say the first time you meet someone, you conclude, "He's a jerk."

Later, as you get to know him, you say, "He's not bad, for a jerk."

Still later, you might say, "When I first met him, I thought he was a Jerk, but he isn't that bad."

And still later, "I like him, even though other people think he's a jerk."

The original judgment of jerkiness will be with him as long as you know him.

The first impressions process is hard wired into our survival mechanism. It isn't logical or even conscious. It's just there—without checks.

A Caveman needed to determine instantly if the man walking into his cave was a friend or foe. He didn't gather data, poll fellow cave dwellers, or create a spreadsheet of probabilities.

No, he judged instantly whether or not to pick up a rock and throw it at the intruder. And while we may not be throwing rocks at ugly people, we judge just as quickly.

It's a response mechanism, part of our survival processes.

The door opens, and you look up, judging instantly whether this person entering is benign or a threat. Will we hug them or hit them?

Your Intendeds have this same instinct. What conclusions are they drawing when they first see you?

And isn't it true that we don't even have four seconds? They see the subject of your email, and decide instantly whether to delete you. They see your post, your tweet, or your logo, and decide in a moment whether to invest a few more seconds into exploring your message.

And even if you survive the first fraction of a second, they will only give you a few more moments to impress them. They may read a bit, but then delete you. And even if you survive a delete, will they act?

It's rare to survive four seconds. And whatever conclusions they arrive at in those four seconds will always be associated with you, even if it is the wrong impression.

In the old days, Cavemen controlled first impressions with their ads, brochures, billboards, jingles, and even websites.

Suitors no longer have this luxury. Intendeds meet you in many different places, hear about you from your Exes, and maybe eavesdrop on your conversations with other Intendeds.

Have you ever been judged by what someone heard you saying out of context as they walk by? How about you? Have you ever made a judgment about someone after hearing a snippet of conversation?

In the Courtship Era, the first impression usually occurs on the Web and in the midst of social media. And in these spaces there is a deluge of messages, many as short as 140 characters.

> *The message many never be heard if the messenger is rejected before he opens his mouth.*

The problem is we often forget that they usually find us from another page, or enter conversations midstream. That is why we need to pay attention to each piece of copy and comment we place in view of Intendeds.

Once they read these messages, it won't matter how attractive you are to them, or how important you could be to their lives; they've already made a judgement, and it will be with you for as long as they are aware of your brand.

So pay attention to first impressions. Pay attention to every piece of copy, message, or any other collateral existing where Intendeds can see you.

I challenge you to randomly click on a page, posting, or tweet from your company. If a person had never heard of you before, what would they think? What would be their first impression of you? What will be sticking with you for as long as they know you. And worse, what will they tell others about you?

They're Already in a Relationship?

L et's face it, all the good ones are taken.

For most companies, their current customers were once customers of someone else. And the really good customers were certainly spending money elsewhere.

Despite what people say, business is a zero-sum game. There is only so much money to be spent, and any market has a finite number of potential customers. It doesn't matter if you have a spectacular emerging technology that everyone in the world will use, it will take decades before everyone owns your product. And by then competition will be so intense that you may not survive long enough to reap the benefits of being first-to-market.

In the business world, it is rare to find a widow from a failed business, or a divorcee from a competitor. Instead, it is usually our job as a Suitor to WOO them away from their current relationship.

Putting social norms and taboos aside, if you saw the love of your life, and she or he were already betrothed to another, wouldn't you at least make a play? Or at least let them know of your interest?

Of course, there are good ways to WOO your Intended away from her current relationship.

Cavemen would simply grab the women away from their competitors. Or attack the competitors, attempting to destroy them, so that customers have no other option but to buy from the Caveman.

And while big companies continue to tear each other apart, Suitors must apply different strategies. And in the Courtship Era, these strategies are not only easier to pull off, they are less destructive.

Why risk a battle that could leave you bloody? Or a campaign that may backfire?

Wouldn't it be better to simply WOO your Intended away from her current supplier?

The route most marketers take, even fledgling Suitors, is to bad-mouth their competition. It is natural to try to assert yourself over your competition, to show how you are better than they are. The problem with this approach is that before she met you, your Intended chose your competitor. And she thought she was making a good choice at the time. By badmouthing your competitors, you are essentially telling your Intended she is stupid.

Your intended wants to stay consistent with her choices. The more you point out the error of her decision, the more entrenched she'll become in her decision.

A better route is to at appear to support her in her decision, but then to ask questions that cause her to doubt her current relationship. Are her needs getting met? Is she getting the attention she deserves? Are there things she wants that she isn't currently getting?

Don't suggest that you can fulfill these lacking points. Your job is to merely ask, and have her tell you her dissatisfactions. You want her to know that if and when things go badly, you are there for her.

For instance, I was once a Land Rover fan. I loved my modified Disco (an insiders' term for the Discover model). I could take that beast anywhere. And I scoffed at people who called their glorified minivans "off-road vehicles." I couldn't even fit into most parking garages because of my suspension and tires.

I was a member of the Land Rover club. We'd go on spectacular trips, and attempt amazing trails. We looked down our noses at other off-road vehicles we saw in the wilderness. We told each other how much better our vehicles were than those people's.

> *When we talk bad about our competition, we talk badly about our prospects' decisions*

But then something happened to the brand. Land Rover ceased to focus on off-roading. Their vehicles became softer and more luxurious. Which was fine in the short term, because my vehicle was from the glory days, when Soccer Mom's weren't allowed to drive these trucks.

And things got worse. I started adding up how much the vehicle was costing to maintain. When I broke it, the repair bill was staggering. I became less happy with my truck. On the outside, of course, I retained all of my bravado. I'd still drive out into the wilderness and drink beer with my Land Rover friends, but I wasn't quite as excited about the experience.

And then Jeep came out with the JK Unlimited, a body long enough to be a true 4-door off-road vehicle. And I switched loyalty seemingly overnight. As soon as the Rubicon version was available, I went to the dealership and ordered mine.

Prior to that decision, if a Jeep owner challenged my choice of a Land Rover, I wouldn't have listened. If they had told me how much better a Jeep was, how much easier it was to maintain, and so on, I would have walked away.

The difference was that I was dissatisfied with my relationship, and all Jeep needed to do was give me a reason to switch. And it came when they gave me enough room in the vehicle to carry all my camping equipment.

And now I have huge loyalty to Jeep. Land Rover can't tempt me back.

And I won't even listen to my friend bragging about his Toyota FJ.

How did Jeep WOO me? First, they provided a product that appealed to me. They were attractive to me. What I needed was a true off-road vehicle that was large enough to carry all my camping gear.

Unlike Land Rover they didn't go after the luxury market with the Wrangler (yes, their other vehicles are too foofy for me). They kept the image that I personify.

And they had the good timing of releasing their new line at exactly the time I was the most dissatisfied with my Land Rover. I didn't want to sink any more money into it.

Could Land Rover have kept me? Maybe.

Could Toyota have WOOed me? Probably.

But Jeep had been around throughout my Land Rover experience. I'd see them on the trails. I'd talk to their owners. Even though I thought I was better than them, they shared with me. When I'd complain, they'd offer insights into their own vehicles.

I would not have listened to Jeep corporate, but I

listened to the people who owned Jeeps. These ambassadors did more to bring me to Jeep than the company did.

So remember that it will be your current customers who WOO your Intendeds away from their current suppliers.

It is always better to have other people praise you than to stand on a hillside beating your own chest. Be available, but let them spread the word.

All you have to do is get your current customers in touch with your Intendeds. And then maybe you'll be able to tempt them away from your competition.

If nothing else, it is a classier move.

EXERCISE: Think about Intendeds already in a relationship with your competitors. What can you do to tempt them away? What problems will they face? What complaints do they have?

_____

_____

_____

_____

_____

_____

_____

_____

_____

_____

_____

_____

_____

_____

_____

_____

_____

_____

_____

_____

You Can't Woo Everyone

In the Little House on the Prairie days we could only appeal to the broadest category of needs and wants. In the television era, we tried to reach as many people as possible. But in the Courtship Era, we must focus on the individual.

The problem is, we aren't trained for this new approach. Most of us were raised on Caveman ways. And we fall into those ways when we are frustrated or confused.

But understand this key point: In the Courtship Era, **when you speak to everyone, you speak to no one.**

In the past, all we could do, or needed to do, was reach as many people as possible with as simple of a message as possible.

But in this new era, our Intendeds expect us to speak to them directly and specifically. They want to be viewed as individuals, not a demographic. They want gifts to be purchased just for them, not recycled from those given to other Intendeds.

The good news is there's a little oddity in English that will help you. We have the same pronoun for second person singular as second person plural: You.

When you use the word *you* in your copy, people feel like you are speaking just to them, even if there are actually a lot of people feeling the same way.

For instance, thousands of people will read this book, yet I use "you." When I do, it feels like I'm engaging you in conversation (well, a monologue), even though I wrote these words a long time ago, and you and I may not have met yet.

It's the same for your Intendeds. When you use *you*, they will feel like you're speaking directly to them, even if this is the first time they've met you. So, whenever you write, whenever you assemble a marketing plan, think in terms of the singular "you."

After all, Intendeds expect you to talk to them directly. General blasts no longer work. Automation feels fake. Sure you can pre-load your Tweets for the week, or plan your posts for the month, but when it comes to talking with them, your Intendeds want to believe they are the only person in front of you.

Think of a deeply in-love couple sharing a meal. Notice how difficult it is for the server to interrupt them.

By contrast, think of a stadium of people watching a game. Some are enthralled. Others are talking. Others are more concerned with their beer and food than the game. Some miss large portions of the game waiting in line at the restroom.

To be a successful Suitor, you want to be that couple at the table, not speaking to the stadium.

The problem is Marketers have been trained to speak to the stadium. We can't resist the bigness of the group, all the potential buyers.

So we broadcast to demographics, say, women between the ages of 25 to 35, with a household income between $50,000 to $75,000, with 1.7 cars, and 2.3 children.

Most people don't want to be most people.

The problem is Intendeds are an exact age, say, 32. And their household income is exact, say, $56,302. And Intendeds probably have one or two cars, not a fraction of one.

And if they have 2.3 children, congratulate them on their pregnancy.

People are not categories; they are individuals.

Let me introduce you to Debbie Diet Coke.

I was told about a television station in San Antonio that realized that a focus on broad demographics doesn't work.

So they invented Debbie Diet Coke.

They knew everything about Debbie. They knew, for instance, her actual age. And since she was a stay-at-home mom, they knew her husband's exact yearly salary. Her minivan was paid off, but the family was making payments on his newer, nicer sedan. They knew how old her two children were, as well as their interests and how well they were doing in school.

They knew everything about Debbie including that she was 15 pounds overweight and she preferred Diet Coke over Diet Pepsi.

Whenever they wrote ad copy, they wrote directly to Debbie Diet Coke. When they had a marketing decision, they asked, "What would Debbie want?" When they made programing choices, they asked, "What would Debbie like to see? What would her husband like to see? And what would they like their kids to see?"

Instead of writing for the whole San Antonio audience, they were reaching a specific person, even though she was fictional.

Now I know what you're thinking, "But what about all the other people watching the station?"

Well, if they were like Debbie, they would feel like they are being spoken too directly.

But what about all those not like Debbie Diet Coke?

Have you ever eves-dropped on someone else's conversation?

Isn't it true that the more different that person was than you, the more interested you were in the conversation?

For example, I have huge brand loyalty to Oakley, and I'm not their target market. Their marketing speaks directly to young, physically-active men.

While I have an adventurous streak, I am not young. And even though I spend a lot of money on Oakley, they refuse to shift their focus to me. And I'm okay with that.

For years now, I have used their Kitchen Sink model of backpack as my office. It's the only backpack they have for a 17-inch Mac. I suspect by the time that you read this, there won't be 17-inch Mac, nor the need for the Kitchen Sink. Regardless, every two years, I have purchased the same bag without even considering other options for carrying my office.

I also wear Oakley sunglasses and ski goggles.

One winter I was skiing at Wolf Creek, CO. If you've been there, you know that there is almost no on-hill lodging. You have to stay miles away from the slopes.

I left before sunrise the first day. I got all the way to the slopes before I realized that I had forgotten my sunglasses. I

> *Don't be tempted away from your type.*

would lose a lot of ski time if I drove back to the hotel for the glasses, so I decided to by a pair of... Oakleys.

Now I didn't need another pair, and I'm not the kind of person who would wear them for a day and return them. My only option was to buy a pair, a nice white pair, and give them to my girlfriend for Christmas.

That's right, I kept the box pristine so that at the end of the day I could clean up the glasses, place them back in the box, wrap the box, and make sure it got under the Christmas tree.

But it got worse. The next day, I had my usual sunglasses, only this day was overcast. When I went into my ski bag, I discovered that I had not only forgotten my goggles, I had evidently also removed my back-up pair as well.

I already have two pair of goggles, which is more than most skiers have, so I didn't need another pair. So there wasn't a logical reason why I would need another expensive pair of Oakley's for the day.

But I did buy the best pair the shop offered. How did I rationalize the purchase? There were plenty of cheaper goggles available. Well, I knew my dad could use a new pair of goggles.

Of course, I didn't give him the new ones. I already had a Christmas gift for him. Instead, I gave him my oldest pair as a hand-me-down. I know, I know. But I really liked the new goggles.

The point is, I have huge brand loyalty for Oakley, I don't hesitate to spend money on them, and yet I'm not their Debbie Diet Coke.

Their website is targeted exclusively to young, physically-active men. Even though they have a women's line, you have to leave their main site and go to a site specifically targeted toward women. Once you're there, you can't get back to the men's side.

Oakley might be tempted to look at my purchasing patterns and begin to market to me, a middle-ager wishing he were young, virile, and athletic. But they don't. They stay true to their Debbie Diet Coke.

And I'm glad they do, because by over-hearing the conversation they have with their Debbies, I feel like I'm crashing an elite and exclusive conversation.

EXERCISE: Consider your marketing efforts. Are you attempting to reach a broad market? Or are you focusing on a specific Intended? Can you describe that person to me?

Below, create your Debbie Diet Coke. Tell me everything about the person down to their drink preferences.

_____

_____

_____

_____

_____

_____

_____

_____

_____

_____

_____

_____

_____

_____

_____

_____

_____

_____

_____

_____

So as we prepare to engage our Intendeds, we must first prepare to leave our homes and go to where they are. We can't wait for them to come to us. We can't expect them to show up where we are. It is our responsibility to go to them.

And we need to make sure that they notice us amid all the other suitors vying for their attention. We have to stand out in the crowd, and heed first impressions.

And then, finally, we must speak just to them. Once we do that, we can mold our conversations to build toward a relationship, instead of leaving them feeling like they are one of many. After all, this is the Courtship Era, and as Suitors, our job is to WOO them.

THE ATTRACTION STAGE

STAGE

It all begins with looking good

It's not about you

Boy sees girl, and falls in love. And then the WOOing begins.

First, he must get her attention, and this is difficult in a flooded market. After all, if he is smitten by her, it's likely others have also been smitten by her, and they are also trying to get her attention and WOO her.

With all these different Suitors, as well as the surviving Cavemen swinging clubs, why will she pick you? How will you stand out in the noisy crowd?

It's not enough to be noticed, you also have to be attractive. You must be what she is looking for once she notices you.

But what do most companies do? They put out there what *they* find attractive, instead of focussing on what their prospects find attractive. They work hard to be attractive to themselves, which makes no sense.

What attracts the Suitor is not what attracts the Intended.

For instance, as a heterosexual male, I find women attractive. I like their look, the shape of their bodies, how their clothes accentuate these qualities, and on and on.

Now, if I put out there what I find attractive, will ladies find me attractive?

In other words, if I dress as a woman, and make up my face as a woman, pad my body, will the women I want find me attractive? (If you want to see what this looks like, friend me on Facebook [facebook.com/jonathan.peters. phd], and check out the 2011 Halloween photos.)

It doesn't work to put out messages that appeal to us. Instead of dressing as we find attractive, we need dress in a manner that our Intendeds find attractive.

But isn't this what most companies do? They put out there what they find attractive, hoping that Intendeds like what they like. Marketers write ads that impress other marketers.

Think of the stereotypical car salesman. He is drawn to sell cars because he likes cars. He reads the magazines, knows the stats, and understands why the car he's selling is a better deal than his competitors'. There's a reason he chose this company to work for.

He also wants to sell cars. He likes the art of selling and negotiation. He reads books, attends seminars, maybe hires coaches. He does all sort of things to be better at sales.

He also likes the lifestyle of sales. He could make money doing any number of things, and he chose car sales.

Does the customer he wants to attract find any of this attractive? Probably not. Sure a few car junkies will wander the lot, and there are a few people who love to get a bargain for a car. But for the most part, prospects just want a car that does what they want, looks the way they want, and that they can afford.

Let's say a potential customer walks onto his lot with the desire to own a new car. Let's say the prospect is a woman who doesn't like the whole negotiation part of car buying. Does she care about the salesman's bonuses and his need to sell her a car to pay his bills? Probably not. And does she care, really, about how the car is engineered and constructed? Maybe. But she's probably most concerned about how she will look in the car, and does it meet her needs.

Now a Caveman would rush her the moment she stepped on the lot, and direct her toward the cars that best fit his perceptions of her needs and budget. He may ask some quali-

> *Your prospects are not like you. If they were, they'd have your job.*

fying questions to know that he is headed in the right direction, but these questions are not designed to get to know her better. Instead, they are part of a script to lead her toward a sale. He wants to direct her.

And once he's decided on what he wants to sell her, he begins the pitch and the close.

And she finds none of this attractive.

It would be better for a Suitor to first provide the product she wants, and to approach the experience from his Intended's perspective. She already knows what she finds attractive, and it is up to the Suitor to either intuit what that is or discover it. She wants to "own" a particular car, not "buy" it. So how can the Suitor be attractive to her?

The intended doesn't want to drive across town to the car lot. And the lot isn't attractive with all the choices crammed next to each other. Many of the models don't interest the Intended.

And it doesn't help that there are balloons, or dancing gorillas, or coffee and hot dogs. That's EW. She just wants to explore her options to find her car.

In fact, the whole car buying process from Caveman days is a real turn-off for consumers.

Wouldn't it be better to approach her in the manner she wants? I'll bet she's already pinned the car, maybe discussed it with her friends, maybe even envisioned herself driving it. Wouldn't it be better if the car salesman met her on Pinterest? And listened to her conversation and questions. What if, instead of being a salesman, he viewed himself as a guide or consultant. Would there be a different relationship between the seller and the buyer? Would the experience be different? And would the pleased customer tell her friends?

So let's quit dressing up in women's clothing, and begin being attractive to our prospects. Let's ask, what do they want? Where are they? And how can we help them make a buying decision.

EXERCISE: Think about your processes. What is EW for your customers? List three things that currently turn off your prospects and customers. Be honest.

_____

_____

_____

_____

_____

_____

_____

_____

_____

SPEED DATING WORKS

It's true, speed dating does work. It conforms to how we make decisions. And best of all, it puts us in front of more potentials than a traditional dating process. We can churn through a lot of potentials without wasting time and money on what isn't going to go anywhere.

How can you choose a potential mate in a manner of seconds? It turns out we are hard-wired to make important decisions instantly. We wouldn't have survived long if it took a day to determine if a Neanderthal were friend or foe, or if the big kitty would purr or eat us, or if fire would be useful or destructive.

Today, we apply this survival skill to all aspects of our lives. When a potential Intended sits down, we note her looks, body movements, and clothes. We hear how she talks, noting her gestures and facial movements. We even smell her.

As un-PC as it may be, and whether you like it or not, we notice people visually, and we judge them visually within seconds of noticing them.

Remember the extremely attractive and the oddly shaped in any crowd? In that split second of noticing them, we also judge them. The oddly shaped, ugly, and shady are negative and should be avoided, while the attractive deserve further investigation.

So not only do we need to be attractive to our Intendeds, they need to notice that attractive element instantly.

This can be difficult if you are not offering a physical product or packaging that can be seen. But it does mean that any time an Intended comes in contact with you, you need to make sure you are visually appealing to her. This could be your advertising and marketing collateral. It could be your website, storefront, or wherever your customers find you.

It is especially true with your logo. The problem is most of our logos are already in place and branded. But it is your logo that is the visual memory for the world. It is the face of your company. You want to make sure it is visually appealing to your Intendeds.

What about posts on social media? It is important to realize that people decide whether to read something or not based on how the document looks, not on the words. In other words, they may never read your words if your post, email, or whatever media you use to send your message, isn't attractive.

You can't do much with Twitter, but the size of your paragraphs impact whether or not an Intended will read your posts. If they're too long, she'll want to read it later.

Then there are the uses of bullets, bolding, and fonts that impact a person's first impression of the post.

Because they are going to judge us from the second they see us, we need to make sure that we are attractive at that moment. If we EW them here, we won't have a chance to WOO them later.

EXERCISE: How do prospects first see your company? What is their first visual impression? Write three negative things that may EW your prospects before they even begin interacting with your company.

_____

_____

_____

_____

_____

_____

_____

_____

_____

What Do Women Want

You may be a fine Suitor. You may be smart, good-looking, have a good future ahead of you, with all those great qualities your mother instilled in you, and you still won't be good enough for your Intended.

Why? Because quality is a given these days. It's the "just friends" territory. You're nice to have around, but your Intended can always get another quality person in her life. She won't commit to you if all you have to offer is what everyone else has.

And here's an insight, what women say they want is often not who they actually end up with. Why? Because what they verbalize they want can be gotten anywhere. It may be attractive, even vital, but it isn't enough to draw them to you.

Anyone can be nice, but only a few can provide them with what they specifically find attractive.

In the marketplace, consumers assume they can get good quality at a good price. And they're willing to pay more for a better product, or sacrifice quality for a lower price. But they don't develop loyalty based on the balance of quality and price. Instead, they base loyalty on something as squishy as preference.

The Intended may find the qualities of a Suitor admirable, but if she doesn't feel that twinge in her heart, he will be stuck as her friend, or worse, a nice guy she once knew.

As a Suitor, your job is to be more than a great guy. You need to be attractive to her. You need to appeal at a heart level to her. And this is difficult to define, much less discover.

It's important to understand that we are talking about emotions here, maybe brain chemistry, but certainly not logic. This is the realm of the heart, and many a hapless man has ignored the heart's importance to relationships.

It's important that you understand how people feel when they do business with you.

Think about it, what does it feel like to shop at a Walmart. Is it different than, say, a Target? Yes, we can look at how the stores are laid out, colors, and so on, but in the end, there is a feeling.

The problem is, you don't know what it's like to be your customers, unless you ask them. And you may also have to visit your competition to make sure you aren't ordinary. Make sure Intendeds can feel a difference when they are engaged with your company and your product.

EXERCISE: I want you to contact your most loyal customers, and ask them what it feels like to do business with you.

In the meantime, identify three characteristics you think define how it feels differently to work with you than your competition.

_____

_____

_____

_____

_____

_____

_____

_____

_____

There is Someone for Everyone

I'm not George Clooney or Brad Pitt. Since I don't display the penultimate of male beauty, does that mean that I am destined to be alone?

Is it possible that even though you aren't the biggest, the best, or the most beautiful that there are still Intendeds who would find you attractive?

For instance, Coca Cola is one of the most ubiquitous brands. They're everywhere. Just painting the stage of *American Idol* in Coca Cola red resulted in more sales for the beverage company. And while Coke is one of the most recognizable brands, a relatively small portion of the human population drinks Coke with any regularity. Yes, many people drink their competitor. But there are even more people who don't like soda at all.

So just because you aren't the biggest company, or even the biggest in your market, it doesn't mean there aren't opportunities to attract Intendeds.

And you don't even have to be the best in your field. I believe Apple produces the best in computers, but there are many people who would disagree. And even those who agree with me, many can't rationalize spending an extra grand for their laptop.

And we don't have to be the most beautiful to be attractive. Porsches are one of the most beautiful production cars, but like the most beautiful woman in the room, very few people approach them. Few can afford them, and of those who can, many find other uses for their money.

So you don't have the be the biggest, the best, or the most beautiful to attract Intendeds. You just have to be attractive to them.

I had to take the picture.

I fumbled in my pocket for my iPhone, juggled it, opened the camera app, and waited for it to load. But by then the tableau had changed.

But in an interesting way.

It all began with my rush to get off the plane at my home airport. It was a Friday. Of course, it is always fun to land in Vegas on Friday night. Beautiful people flood into the city on weekends. So any plane coming to Vegas from anywhere is going to have a disproportionate number of beautiful people on it.

But my rush to get off the plane on this Friday night was blocked by two large people holding hands, thus taking up the whole tunnel leading from the plane into the terminal.

The man was short and very round, and his legs only moved his body forward a couple inches at a time. As far as looks go, Dilbert was his better-looking brother.

The lady towered with staggering dimensions in all directions. She leaned sideways to grasp the man's hand, and moved awkwardly to match her strides to his.

The site of them kept me from noticing the 120 normal and beautiful people leaving the plane with me. All I noticed was this couple.

And they were in love.

I mean really in love. The kind you rarely see in public.

And I wanted to take a picture of it.

But during all my fumbling, even the lady got frustrated with their progress and the crush of people piling up behind them. Without a word, she discarded the man's hand and stomped up the gangplank and into the terminal.

> Statistically speaking, half of your market is below average. While others are chasing the ideal customer, there are plenty of other opportunities with the rest of the group.

By the time I got the camera ready to take the picture, I could only move abreast of the man to take his shot.

It was then that I looked up and saw the woman pausing in the flow of people to look back at her man with love in her eyes, oblivious of the people pushing past her and around her man.

And I thought, not only is there someone for everyone, the more specialized they are, the less likely they are to notice anyone else. Beauty really is in the eye of the beholder.

That man, as round and as unattractive as the rest of us found him, had something few of us have. He enjoyed an intensity of love that most poeple never experience in life.

And somehow they found each other.

And they were perfect for each other. I'm pretty sure no other man on that plane would find the woman attractive. And the man certainly didn't turn any heads. But they only had eyes for each other. In fact, they didn't notice the other people, those we consider to be more beautiful.

Studies have shown that while we do have some general standards of what constitutes a beautiful human, people are attracted to their "level."

For instance, a man who ranks a 5 will find women in the 6 to 7 range attractive, and he will pursue them. While a man who is an 8 won't even notice the women in the lower range.

More interestingly, the 5 man has no interest in the 9 or 10 woman.

Another way of looking at this phenomenon is the interactions between Alpha and Beta types.

In most social groups, Alpha status will be fought over between about 10% of the group. Beta status will be roughly the next 20% to 30%. The rest make up followers, and we can call them Theta.

When it comes to social interaction, dating, even friendships, Alphas will pursue Alphas. Betas probably will not approach Alphas. For instance, Beta men may look at an Alpha woman, but they won't engage her in conversation unless she speaks to them first. Interestingly, Beta women will save the Alpha man for the Alpha woman, even if she is not present.

This means there is actually a larger market in the Beta range, because not only will the Betas talk with the Betas, but so will the Thetas who look up to the Betas and consider the Alphas out of their league.

So not only are we programed to interact with those in our league, it may actually hurt us if we are the biggest, the best, or the most beautiful. When we hold a dominant position in the market, we may actually have a smaller customer pool.

Yes, the biggest, best, and most beautiful get the most attention, and people may admire them, but when it comes to relationships, there are more fish in the Beta sea.

This also means there is nothing wrong with acknowledging that you aren't the biggest, best, or most beautiful. Take Avis for instance. For 13 consecutive years they lost money. Then they changed their marketing language to "Avis is only No. 2 in rent-a-cars. So why go with us? We try harder." From that point, they began to make money? Why? Because only a few of us feel worthy of number one (Hertz, in this case), but all of us can interact with number two.

> *Who loves you? That is your market. Don't chase someone else's love.*

While Beta status may be the safest, there are even opportunities in the Theta, as Dilbert's brother getting off the plane taught me. Dilbert's brother had a woman who loved him, and I slept alone that night.

In the Courtship Era, let the Alpha companies beat each other up to prove who's the biggest, best, and most beautiful. While they attack each other, begin interacting with Intendeds. Approach them, talk with them, invite them to join you for coffee. Soon, they will be loyal customers. Who wants to deal with the egos of Brad Pitt or George Clooney anyway?

EXERCISE: Let's be serious about your market position. List the biggest companies in your market:

1. _____

2. _____

3. _____

List the best companies in your market:

1. _____

2. _____

3. _____

List the most beautiful companies in your market:

1. _____

2. _____

3. _____

What qualities do you offer that the biggest, the best, and
the most beautiful don't?

_____

_____

_____

_____

_____

_____

_____

_____

_____

_____

_____

_____

_____

_____

_____

_____

_____

_____

_____

_____

_____

Looks Get You in the Door, Personality Keeps You There

Yes, good looks attract. That is why our marketing collateral must be attractive, must appeal to our Intendeds, and must keep our image in their minds. But what keeps them engaged?

Our personality.

You know that stunningly beautiful person who is a total air head, or ass, or bitch? You were attracted to them because they were beautiful, but you were repulsed by them because of their personality.

An Intended may pay attention to the peacock, but to stay in the game, you must have a personality that is also attractive. What appears as self-confidence to the Alphas comes across as arrogance to the Betas. And the personality that attracts you, may not attract them. A quality that you find admirable, they may find mundane.

So once again, it is important that you be attractive to your Intended, not to yourself.

It is important that we understand that personality is not about identity. He may be a member of the band, hold a key position, or be in commercials, but that says little of who he is. Identity is merely about his place in the group.

African American is an identity. Doctor is an identity. High IQ or high wealth is an identity. All of these identities are important for the first stage of attraction, but their power only lasts a few moments.

Personality is that part of people that makes them different from others who look like them. It's what makes them them. It's the qualities that people relate to, converse with, and laugh along with. And since it is unique to each Suitor, it is difficult to describe.

Take airline personalities as an example. Besides mileage on different airlines, I have little emotional attachment with most of them. Yes, I have stories about bad experiences on some (American and US Airways), and I don't like flying on them. But if they could get me from here to there more cheaply than the airlines I do like, I might find myself on one of their planes.

But there are certain airlines that emerge out of the neutral category to be a preference airline for me. For instance, because of my status on United, I often fly first class for coach fare. I appreciate that. Hot meals on Hawaiian Air are nice. The quirks of Alaska Air make them an interesting experience.

But I do have an emotional connection to, and a loyalty for, Southwest Airlines. Yes, they are convenient for me. And they offer a free checked bag, which at my level of travel, isn't as big of a deal; I have enough status on other airlines to get free bags. And the ease of switching flights does fit my ever-changing schedule. But what creates my loyalty is their personality. I mean when was the last time the airline attendants officiated a game involving toilet paper that pitted one side of the plane against the other?

Now that's personality.

So while Marketers often focus on our look, in the Courtship Era we must put even more emphasis on our personality. Because good looks will get the attention of our Intendeds, but they cannot move us into the different stages of a relationship.

Without a personality, you may get customers. With an objectionable personality you will repel prospects.

You've heard women complain that there aren't any good men. Or that all the good ones are taken. They don't mean that there aren't any good looking men available; they are saying that all the men they meet do not have attractive personalities.

Your Intendeds may be saying the same thing about your market niche. Your competitors may look good. They may be the biggest, the best, or the most beautiful, and you can still beat them on personality.

EXERCISE: Pretend you are writing a post for your company on a dating site. What would you say?

_____

_____

_____

_____

_____

_____

_____

_____

_____

_____

But Not Just Any Personality

Isn't it true that your friends' personalities are similar to yours? The reason you can communicate so well with them is because they understand you.

But are your friends also your Intendeds?

And isn't it also true that your Intendeds communicate well with their friends?

So the key is to figure out how to match your personality to theirs.

Perhaps you're familiar with the personality styles. The idea that there are four basic types of people has been around for centuries. Many attribute Hypocrites with the first observation of these characteristics, but he was actually arguing that instead of being guided by the elements (Earth, Wind, Fire, Water), we are guided by the different body fluids (Phlegmatic, Choleric, Sanguine, and Melancholy).

Over the centuries, people have examined and expanded on the importance of the personality styles. For our purposes, consider that your Intended's personality style is probably different from your own. And since your job is to attract her, it is your responsibility to present yourself in a way that, well, attracts her.

How about a quick summary? I'll be using labels for the different personality styles that I'm familiar with. They are descriptive terms. Realize that there are many different systems, and therefore many different terms. The good thing is that all systems basically agree.

VISIONARY: GET IT DONE

Visionaries are goal oriented. They are primarily concerned with opportunity and time. They are competitive, quick to act, and like to take risks. Details get in the way, and your silly emotions and stories slow things down. Also, with the assurance of their convictions, once they make a decision, they don't want to continue to discuss options.

Visionaries don't like small talk. Instead of social niceties, Visionaries appreciate concise communication. They want you to simply state your opinion or what you want. They know it is raining, and they don't want to discuss their family or their golf handicap with you. They aren't being rude; they simply want to get down to business.

But don't mistake this attitude with a desire for logical, passionless business discussions. Visionaries expect you to be enthusiastic about selling your product. They will become suspicious if you show even the slightest lack of confidence in yourself, your sales pitch, or your product.

This means the best approach is to tell them how you will solve their problems, and then get more detailed if they want. Watch for cues that a Visionary has made up their mind. You may have a lot more features and benefits to discuss, but the Visionary may have already anticipated what you are going to say, and already made a decision. At that point, they don't want to hear any more from you.

Characteristics of a Visionaries

Grounded in convictions

Passionate

Focused on goals

Concerned with time to completion

Enterprising

Innovative

Ambitious

Driven

Risk-taker

Quick to act

Competitive

Expressing a lot of emotional energy

Unconcerned with the status quo

Self-confident

Persuasive

ANALYTICALS: GET IT DONE RIGHT

Analyticals love information and details. They tend to be logical people who investigate facts and question processes. Their desks are orderly, and they have a systematic process for doing even the most ordinary tasks. They prefer technological solutions, and they are the people to go to when you have a question.

Details have meaning for Analyticals. They discover possibilities through research and make decisions based on an investigation of the facts. Because of this characteristic, Analyticals view summaries as wastes of time.

Since Analyticals possess more knowledge and detail than the average person, they tend to be self-reliant. They have their routines and are cautious.

When you are selling to Analyticals, make sure you are well prepared. You need to know every bit of information about your product because they will also want to know about the processes and even your delivery system long before they begin to consider making a purchasing decision. They will wear you out with their questions, and read every word you write, including the owner's manual.

Don't rush them or push them. They will continue to ask for details until you have made them feel confident in your product. Analyticals will want time to analyze the benefits and features of your product, and you can expect them to compare your product to others'.

Analyticals will be suspicious if you engage in too much small talk, or if you gloss over details.

Characteristics of a Analyticals

Detailed

Systematic

Factual

Orderly

Self-reliant

Organized

Cautious

Reserved

Methodical

Principled

Fair

Preserving

COACHES: GET ALONG

Coaches are characterized by their concern for others. They care about the well-being of those around them. They are team-players, and seek to bring out the best in others. Better yet, they are accepting of others, accommodating, and compassionate. You couldn't ask for a better friend.

Coaches seek consensus. For instance, when it comes to choosing a place to eat, Coaches will make sure everyone's tastes and dietary limitations are taken into account before deciding on a restaurant. And they won't make fun of anyone's dislikes. Coaches strive to protect everyone's feelings while reaching a consensus.

Coaches like small talk. To feel comfortable with you, and to trust what you have to say, they want to get to know you as a person. And they appreciate your efforts to get to know them.

Once you establish a strong working relationship with a Coach, you can expect them to remain loyal to you. As long as you don't hurt the relationship, it will be difficult for your competition to take business away from you. As your relationship develops, Coaches will confide in you. You will learn about the needs of the company, and you will pick up clues for gaining additional business.

Coaches need to consult others to feel confident in their decisions. Should you push them, they will not do business with you. Give them testimonials, recommendations, and suggest they consult with others.

Better yet, tell them how your product will benefit others. Coaches feel better about products that help others or are good for the environment, and they like to know that suppliers give back to the community. Probably the worst thing you can do with a Coach is to suggest some sort of kickback.

The main thing is to not get frustrated with how long it takes Coaches to make a decision. Stick with it, and they will be your loyal customer.

Characteristics of a Coaches

> Devoted
>
> Collaborator
>
> Concerned for others
>
> Team player
>
> Sensitive to the feelings of others
>
> People-centered
>
> Trusting
>
> Loyal
>
> Helpful
>
> Modest

PROMOTERS: GET RECOGNITION

Promoters are flexible and open to options. They are tolerant of different types of people, and they are able to accept multiple viewpoints. Because they are flexible and have many coping tools, Promoters adjust easily to changing conditions. In fact, they like change.

They are problem-solvers who seek multiple options and possibilities. In their efforts to solve problems, Promoters do not like to be limited by rigid systems, rules, or time constraints. And they don't like to be separated from others who might be sources of information and insight.

If you are a Promoter, you probably find it easy to get along with different types of people. You are able to consider different opinions and beliefs without being threatened. You probably like change and get bored easily with routine. You feel comfortable with experimenting before making a decision, and even after you have made a decision, you will remain open to the possibility that better opportunities may appear.

Promoters, by their nature, are harder to figure out when you first meet them. You may at first peg them as Coaches because of their willingness to engage you in conversation. You may then think they are a Visionary when they grasp the broader view of what you have to offer. And you may think they are Analyticals when they ask you about the specifics of your product. But when they ask about options, you will finally recognize them.

Promoters, while sociable and accommodating, can be frustrating. They are constantly looking for options and questioning established methods for doing something. If you have a cylinder that fits in a round hole, they will question why the hole is round in the first place. Even after they have made a decision to purchase your product, they will continue to look for alternatives, and they will often ask you to compare your product to your competition.

Promoters will expect you to present the pros and cons of your product. They will ask you about alternatives and push you to examine other possibilities. They may ask you to consider another option and then come back later to present your findings. Sometimes they will want detailed explanations and other times they will not.

Promoters do not like rules. Don't tell them that things have to be done a certain way or by a certain time. If you attempt some sort of Caveman pitch, such as "buy today or the price will go up," it is likely that the Promoters will shrug their shoulders. Worse, they may resent you for such tactics.

The quickest way to lose a sale with Promoters is to tell them that it cannot be done. If they figure out that it can, in fact, be done, they will not trust you in the future.

If you are not a Promoter, you may find Promoters wishy-washy. On one day, one thing will be important, and a totally different thing will be important on the next. You will think you are selling them one product, but they will be more interested in something else you offer.

You may want to present certain features and benefits, but Promoters may cut you off and ask seemingly unrelated questions. However, if you can put up with Promoters, they will explain what they need and how you can solve their needs.

Characteristics of a Promoter

Flexible

Problem solver

Adaptable

Embraces change

Tolerant

Accommodating

Friendly

Sociable

Experimenter

Seeks options

IT'S NOT THAT EASY

Of course, people don't fall nicely into four categories. We have many different influences and experiences that have also formed us.

While we do comply to one of the four personality styles, we also have a secondary one that modifies our responses and experiences.

Beyond our primary and secondary personality influences, we also grow up in a generation. And generations have personality styles of their own.

And then there are the motivators that you'll hear about in a few pages.

And then life happens.

It can all get complicated. It is important to understand that while we can assume a lot about people by when they are born and the characteristics they display, we must still focus on the individual. Any lumping that we might be tempted to do will hurt our relationship with our Intendeds. The point of learning about personalities, generational influences, motivators, and so on, is to help us communicate with our Intendeds.

In the end, we can't control them. We can only seek to understand them better, so that we can communicate with our Intendeds better, and give them what they want.

WHAT IF YOU DON'T KNOW THEM YET

I know what you're thinking, "What if I don't know what type of personality I'm dealing with?"

Well, ask.

And if you're reaching many different people, make sure you provide the types of interactions they all want.

Give a clear ROI to Visionaries.

Make sure details are on your website, and that you provide sources for any information and studies you site for the Analyticals.

Coaches will want testimonials.

And you'd better have fun and interesting marketing collateral for your Promoters.

But let's drill a little deeper. Who is your target Intended?

High-value decision makers tend to be Visionary because of their vision and drive. They might also be Promoters because of their affability.

If you have a high-end product or want to reach decision makers, keep your value proposition simple. Too much information, too early, will frustrate Visionaries. Simply tell them how your product can get them to where they want to go. Then sit back and listen.

The great thing is if you make a good case, the sale will be quick and easy.

Promoters are similar, but you have to be fun and interesting. You also have to be cool enough to be associated with them. Anything short of the best won't work. Appeal to their image of themselves. Remember, this is not about you. If your Intended is a Promoters, make sure she feels like you are a complement to her. You need to look good on her arm.

But remember, as soon as a cuter Suitor comes along, you may lose her. So make sure you constantly make her feel important and special, and make sure you are exclusive. If anyone can get you, she'll see you as common, and go looking for another boy-toy.

Bring flowers to the Coach. Share with her how you've helped others. Don't flatter her, but be open and supportive of her. She will take a long time to decide, and she'll want to ask her friends about you, maybe want her father's permission to date you. She will feel guilty if you are a luxury. And she'll need to be assured over and over that you care.

And the Analyticals, if they're your Intended, God bless you. As Marketers, we tend to be Promoters; some of us are Coaches because of the products or services we're bringing to the market. If you've made it this far into this book, you're probably not a Visionary (my style is too ethereal for them). But I would put money down, big money down, more than the price of this book, that you are not an Analytic (unless you are my proofreader).

As marketers, Analyticals frustrate the hell out of us. We must provide them the information that we haven't bothered to assemble. And it takes them so long to reach a decision, that we often walk away before they decide.

And yet, if you are the best choice, the logical choice, it's worth the long courting process.

And realize this, a good Visionary or Promoter will rely on an Analytical to make important recommendations. Sure the Visionary or Promoter may be the ultimate decider, but you may have to pass the Analytical test first.

> *Don't try to be what you're not, but appeal to who they are.*

Think of the Analytical as a skeptical father. You've put on the charm, shown your benefits, and professed your love for her. Then her father steps in, and you realize you've blown it. Often, it's worth getting the Analytical father on your side first; you can WOO the Intended later.

All of this assumes you are speaking to an individual, and I hope that you are speaking to your Debbie Diet Coke. But you should also consider that any marketing campaign should have all four elements in it: a clear ROI, details, testimonials, and good-looking marketing elements.

Remember, your job as a Suitor is to bend to them, to provide marketing collateral that appeals to them. And be ready to begin a relationship with them. Court them the way they want to be courted.

EXERCISE: Identify the elements of your marketing plan that reach out to each of the four personality styles.

Visionary _____
_____
_____
_____
_____
_____

Analytical _____
_____
_____
_____
_____

Coach _____
_____
_____
_____
_____

Promoter _____
_____
_____
_____
_____

So You Think You've Got Game

Well, you're just beginning.

Once you know her personality style, then you need to figure out what motivates your Intended because she will not buy until she is sufficiently motivated.

Have you noticed that people don't get excited about the same things you do?

Did you know that some people actually prefer Michelob Ultra?

As I write these words I'm sitting in a brewery on the ocean in California (they didn't pay me for a mention). Of all the wonderful beers available, even wheats and heffs, and all the amazing liquors, the guys behind me just ordered Bud Lights.

Really?

Why would anyone come to this place to order shit-beer? And, oddly enough, because it's happy hour, they paid just as much for their beer as I did for my amazingly crafted stout.

I've just had three beers that I've never sampled before. They chose beer they could have had anywhere in America. Am I right, and they're wrong?

Well, yes. Of course I believe I'm right. But then again, I'm differently motivated then they are. They want their usual, because that's what they always have. Even if the location is different, they return to the familiar.

As for me, I came here because I could have a beer here that is not served anywhere else in the world. That very fact drives me.

The problem is we naturally believe our motivations are correct. And when people are differently motivated than we are, we assume they are wrong. But they also assume they are right and we're wrong.

Steven Reiss of Ohio State University documented 16 core motivators. All of us have our own combination of these motivators. Some of the 16 are chief motivators for us, others are neutral, and still others are low motivators.

Think of a scale from one to ten. Of the 16 motivators, three or four will rank close to 10. And three and four will hover closer to one or two. The rest hover in the middle of the scale.

The problem, again, is that we believe our combination is the correct one, and that other combinations are wrong.

For instance, let's say a psychologist is uncomfortable with the randomness of human emotions, so he studies psychology to put order to what he perceives as irrational behavior. There is also the problem of people making choices that are not in their best interest. And then there are those random oddities of humanity. The psychologist wants to put all of these behaviors in a box because he is motivated by order. He wants to minimize chaos in his life and the world around him.

And then the psychologist bumps into this guy who lives life on the road. This guy thrives while sleeping in a different hotel room every night. He loves new experiences, meeting strangers, and is averse to visiting the same restaurant or bar more than once, unless he is taking friends to the different places he's discovered.

He doesn't have any traditional family ties like a wife and kids. Worse, he doesn't seem to desire them or need them.

Since order is not a motivator of this patient, the patient must be wrong and need medication.

It's not about what you want them to do, but what will motivate them to take action.

For his part, the patient thinks the psychologist has something wrong with him because he is so bound by his practice and routines that he can't really enjoy life. The psychologist eats at the same chain restaurant every Friday night, has the same lunch every day. And he always watches certain shows on certain nights. With so much to enjoy in life, how can a healthy person choose a life of quiet desperation?

The truth is neither man is wrong; they are just differently motivated.

So how does this relate to the Suitor and his Intended? She is probably differently motivated.

Consider this, you chose your field of work and the company you work for. You chose the uncertainties of marketing and business. It is your job to find new and different ways to communicate with your Intendeds.

By contrast, your Intended didn't make any of these choices. They are differently motivated than you. In fact, they have little that is like you.

This is why some of the most creative ad campaigns fall flat. Why? Because they are constructed to impress Suitors instead of Intendeds. And audiences aren't impressed, nor do they care about your creativity.

As the Suitor, it is your responsibility to discover what motivates your intendeds, and work with those motivators. They are not wrong because they are motivated differently than you, and they will not change just because you want them to.

The motivators are rooted in our survival instincts. Again, each of us has three or four that are major motivators, that drive us away from what we don't want and toward what we do want. And there are three or four motivators that, while rooted in our survival tendencies, do not have much of an impact in our lives. In fact, our low motivators may actually be de-motivators in our daily lives.

As you read the different descriptions of these motivators, note your three or four chief motivators and which ones don't have much of an impact in your life. But more important, consider the motivators of your Intendeds. Remember, it is your responsibility to be attractive to them.

EATING: THE NEED FOR FOOD

We all need food; it is core to our survival. But for some people eating is a chief motivator. They get up thinking about food. When they're done with one meal, they begin thinking about the next. In case you think that only the obese are motivated by food, there are also people who truly enjoy food. They may eat sensibly, and even be in shape, and yet, when they eat, they thoroughly enjoy eating, and plan their next meal as soon as they are done with the current one.

People who are motivated by food view themselves as connoisseurs, happy, sensual, even gourmands.

On the other hand, people who are not motivated by food look down on those who are motivated by eating. They believe food-motivated people are impulsive and weak willed. Meanwhile, these non-eaters view themselves as healthy, sensible, and fit.

You know these people. They examine their food to the point where they can't enjoy the sensual aspect of food. They are so worried about the properties of the food, they don't appreciate the flavor, texture, and aroma. And they feel superior in their non-appreciation of food.

Each group member believes they are the better person and either looks down on or feels sorry for the other.

So let's say you are not highly motivated by eating, yet your Intendeds are. You might not think about it, but they would be highly attracted to you if you brought them donuts, or gave them gift cards to restaurants. As Suitors, it is our job to cross the divide, and take them out on a date.

EXERCISE: How can you use the eating motivator to market your company? _____

_____

_____

_____

_____

_____

ROMANCE: THE NEED FOR SEX

Sex is a biological drive, and we are wired to desire it. And for many marketers sex or romance is a high motivator. The problem is in our rush to portray what attracts us, we repel and EW many of our Intendeds who have a low drive for sex. They are turned off by sexual images or implications. Even this subject's appearance in this book makes them uncomfortable.

While they have physical desires for sex, they may be repelled by those desires because they are counter to other motivators.

Those who are not motivated by romance and sex view themselves as virtuous, spiritual, even cerebral. They are proud that they are not controlled by base desires.

Meanwhile, those who are motivated by sex and romance view themselves as sensitive and flirtatious. They also feel they are controlled in the midst of their high sex drive and romantic pursuits. Once again, they can't understand why someone would deny themselves something that gives so much enjoyment and meaning in life.

An interesting aside, high-wealth and successful people often have sex and romance as a high motivator. Just think about the scandals.

As important and enjoyable as sex is, as a motivator, romance and sex often causes a divide between Suitors and Intendeds. Find out first if your Intended is motivated by sex and romance before you throw up suggestive images, hire sexy models, and throw around innuendos.

EXERCISE: How can you use the romance motivator and the need for sex to market your company? _____

_____

_____

_____

_____

_____

FAMILY: THE NEED TO RAISE CHILDREN

Again, we all have the biological drive to reproduce. It's what keeps the species going. The problem is some of us are motivated by this desire, and others think having children would be nice except the ones screaming behind them in the airplane. The more that brat kicks the back of the seat on the night flight to Hawaii, the more thankful they are that they don't have children and the more they wished others had just kept their legs crossed or pulled out in time. Or maybe take responsibility for their brats. (Glad I got that off my chest. Where were we?)

On the other hand, if you are motivated by the need to raise children, you feel sorry for the kid on the airplane, and her parents having to comfort the little lady. Planes, after all, are so hard on children.

If you are dedicated to your career, trying to get to the next level, focussed on your financial goals, it is likely that family is not a high motivator. This doesn't mean that you don't love your spouse and children. It does mean, how-ever, that you are occasionally late to family events, maybe even miss a soccer game or three. You probably also don't see a problem with hiring a babysitter so that you and your spouse can have a romantic evening (especially if romance and sex are motivators).

If you're reading this book, I'm assuming that family is not one of your top three motivators. Yes, you love your family; that's not the point. As a motivator, the need to raise children may be a seven on the ten scale, and other motivators are driving your activities. You don't need to feel guilty, it's just how you're wired.

Those with a high family motivator simply work to pro-vide shelter and food for their family. They are not trying to build a business, reach new markets, or even improve themselves professionally. They are satisfied with stable jobs that require the least amount of hours to get the max-imum benefits. Their career goals are based on providing more for their families and setting up a solid retirement. They have plenty of insurance and avoid activities that might result in needing that insurance.

They usually aren't attracted to the field of marketing.

The problem is your Intendeds probably are motivated by family and the need to raise children. Even if it isn't a chief motivator of yours, it does impact the decisions they make.

But notice how many ads fail to include children in their message. You may see a couple enjoying luxury, or a woman displaying her wonderful hair, but unless your company and product appeals to family and children, you probably aren't reaching out to those who are motivated by their family and the need to raise children.

EXERCISE: How can you use the family motivator and the need to raise children to market your company?

_____

_____

_____

_____

_____

TRANQUILITY: THE NEED TO BE SAFE

We all have a need to feel safe, at least some of the time, but some people are highly motivated by tranquility. They want their environment to not only be quiet and peaceful, but they also want assurance that it will remain the same in the future.

These Intendeds are careful, cautious, and prudent. They are wary of making a bad decision. They prize the status quo, as long as it is not disruptive or disharmonious. This means they are satisfied with their current Suitor, if he serves their needs. And even if there are disruptions in their life, the tranquility motivated will be shy about seeking you out.

This means the tranquility motivated must first be aware of you, but not in a loud or obvious way. If you seek to attract a tranquility motivated Intended, quietly let her know you are there for her when she needs you. Show her how you will keep her life quiet and even. Also, make sure you tell her how you'll prevent disruptions in her future. You must be consistent and conscientious.

The best way to attract a tranquility motivated Intended is to become part of her current routine. Make it easy for her to switch suppliers. Assure her at each stage, and take it slowly. Think about snuggling in front of the TV on a Saturday night, like you have every Saturday for the last 50 years. That's the image you want to project for tranquility motivated people.

EXERCISE: How can you use the tranquility motivator and the need to feel safe to market your company?

BELONGING: THE NEED FOR FRIENDS

We need people in our lives to survive. And we certainly enjoy spending time with friends. But for some, their friends are very important to them, so much so that social contact is a prime reason for their actions and choices. They want to spend time in the company of others.

If your Intended is motivated by belonging, the best thing to do is provide a place where she can have that contact, not necessarily with you, but with her friends. Of course this could be a physical space like a restaurant or bar, but it can also be a virtual space. Social media has given marketers tools to help attract Intendeds motivated by social contact.

Think of the quick rise of Pinterest. What did they do? Provide a virtual space where people can share what they find interesting. There is a sense of community as I post what I like, and snoop on what others find interesting. The whole point of the space is to have social contact at least to a point. Social media doesn't replace social contact for those motivated by peer relationships, but it does extend their contact, thus intensifying their exposure to their friends.

Regardless of how your Intendeds are motivated, you should be reaching out through social media, but if you're intendeds are motivated by social contact, consider creating spaces where they can interact with their peers. Don't be so egotistical to think that you are their friend. They might like talking with you, but you are a Suitor. You want a different relationship with them.

While we all need social contact to survive, remember that there are people for whom belonging is a one or a two on the motivator meter. They would rather spend a night at home alone with a bowl of ice cream, or in the woods hiking over a ridge, or on a secluded island, than chatting in your Facebook group.

These people don't care about your random thoughts, nor do they want to see pictures of what someone ate for dinner. It is important to realize that while you are probably motivated by social contact, some people are irritated by your chatter. If your Intendeds are not motivate by social contact, do not force them to have conversations with you. Leave them alone. They'll come to you when they are ready.

EXERCISE: Okay, this one might be easier for you. How can you use the belonging motivator to market your company? _____

_____

_____

_____

_____

_____

PHYSICAL ACTIVITY: THE NEED FOR

EXERCISE

Yes, it's true; some people really are motivated by physical activity. But it's just as true that many people have a low motivation for physical activity, especially after years of sitting in a cubicle. Yet physical activity is part of our survival mechanism. We have a need to move away from danger. And for some, this motivator is a nine or a ten.

The thing to remember with this motivator is not so much the tendencies of those who are motivated by it (we understand those), but of those who are not motivated by exercise. These people do not view themselves as lazy. Instead, they are proud of their laid-back nature. They don't feel bad about being low key and easy going.

Of course, the extremely motivated by physical activity scorn these low key people. If you have tendencies toward physical activity, be careful about your attitude toward Intendeds who would rather spend an evening on the couch than a Saturday on a bike. If they feel like you are looking down on them, they will ignore you. They don't like to feel your distain.

Similarly, check the images you use in your marketing. Climbing up a hillside to see a beautiful view is not only uninteresting to non-exercise motivated people, they believe such experiences are miserable.

You would do better to have slower-paced video, casual text, and voice-overs that talk in slower drawls. Such collateral may be abhorrent to you, but your goal is to attract your Intended, not prove how vigorous and athletic you are.

Of course, if your Intended is motivated by physical

activity, you'd better have fast images, show challenging activities, and make sure they don't see anyone sitting around, drinking sugar drinks... unless you are Mountain Dew.

EXERCISE: How can you use the physical activity motivator to market your company? _____

_____

_____

_____

_____

ACCEPTANCE: THE NEED FOR APPROVAL

We all want to be accepted. In ancient times our survival was based on the group accepting us. We want our peer group to like us. But some people are more motivated by acceptance than others. And many people couldn't care less what other people think about them.

The biggest conflict with the acceptance motivator occurs in the boss/employee relationship. A driven person, especially a business owner or entrepreneur, does not have a high motivation for acceptance; otherwise, they wouldn't have taken the steps needed to get ahead.

The problem arises when their employees are motivated

by acceptance. They want to be appreciated for their contribution. There is nothing they prize more than a simple "thank you" from the boss.

And yet, bosses won't give it. Not because they aren't appreciative, not because they don't like their employee, they just simply aren't motivated by acceptance, and they expect others to be the same as them.

Acceptance folks go with the group. They don't like standing out. They won't risk disdain from others.

Those not motivated by acceptance view themselves as self-assured, persistent, and confident. They see those needing acceptance as weak.

But again, your Intended probably wants to be appreciated. She wants you to acknowledge her, prize her, even praise her. Caveman techniques often manipulate this motivator. If you don't buy this soap, your husband won't appreciate you. If you don't buy this cereal for you kids, they won't love you. Without this car, your neighbors will wish you would move to a different neighborhood.

In the short term, we can manipulate acceptance motivated people, but over time, we abuse our relationship with them. At some point, they will leave us for someone who does appreciate them.

It would be better to praise people. Thank customers, compliment Intendeds. Even if they are not particularly motivated by acceptance, they will appreciate that you are paying attention to them.

EXERCISE: How can you use the acceptance motivator

to market your company? _____

_____

_____

_____

_____

STATUS: THE NEED FOR SOCIAL STANDING/IMPORTANCE

Marketers love status motivated people. Why? Because they allow us to produce some fun collateral. We get to portray the lifestyle people dream of. We need images and footage of beautiful people doing fun things. We may even get to work with celebrities. And if we play the budgets right, we can visit exotic locations.

That is, unless we are only the copywriters, or if budgets are so low that we have to use stock footage.

The point is status people want to associate themselves with the beautiful, the prominent, and the prestigious. To attract them, we have to demonstrate to them how our products will help them get that lifestyle, or at least cause others to believe that they already have the lifestyle.

Status motivated people spend a lot to look good. Even in their bargain shopping, they'll still pay way beyond what is practical. A bag shouldn't cost that much simply because it has a certain logo on it. You probably will never drive a car faster than 80 miles per hour. And who needs a watch anymore?

A status motivated Intended wants to feel important.

She believes she is worthy of your recognition. She enjoys your flattery, even while she questions your sincerity. In your marketing you simply must demonstrate how important she'll be when she is associated with your product. And make sure only certain people have the opportunity to acquire your product. Oddly, make sure you overcharge for your product. Even if she later buys at a discount, at least others will believe she paid full price.

In their effort to be seen as attractive, to be noticed, status Intendeds draw the attention of a lot of Suitors. After all, these Intendeds spend more than they should to look good. So you will have a lot of competition when you pursue status motivated Intendeds. Each one of them will be waving their wears, attempting to attract the attention of your Intended. Maybe they were able to align themselves with the right celebrity. Maybe they have a community of high-value people displaying their logo. Maybe they are perceived as being more exclusive.

It's a tough field where you have to both be available to your Intended while appearing to not be available to people she feels better than. You need to charge enough to make people believe you are a luxury brand, but not so much that you are outside the range of your Intended. It's a difficult and treacherous balancing act working with status motivated Intendeds.

If you do attract the status motivated Intended, you will have her loyalty. After all, she can't appear wrong in her own eyes. If she owns your product now, she will want to believe that you continue to have value and name recognition. The only real danger is that she finds your competitor to be more prestigious than you, or that she believes that she will look better with your competitor's product.

The status motivated intended is not fickle, just always looking for a better Suitor. You may be all she can afford now, but when she gets to the next stage she will be able to afford something more prestigious. And she's looking forward to that time.

Of course some people are not motivated by status. These people won't be irritated by your marketing to the status motivated. They will simply have a dim view of you and your Intended. They will see your status motivated Intended as shallow, wasteful, and irresponsible. They will see you as taking advantage of the gluttony or greed of others.

Those not motivated by status see themselves as practical and fair minded. They care about others. They want to know what you have done to make things better for the less fortunate. They want to hear stories about how you rescued a puppy, comforted a crying child, and saved a whale.

They won't be impressed by your logo. They want the best price for the quality. Logos only service you if you have a reputation for quality. But you'd better not be flashy or gregarious.

There are opportunities on both sides of the status motivator, though it can be more fun to pursue a status motivated Intended, especially if you are similarly motivated.

EXERCISE: How can you use the status motivator to

market your company? _____

_____

_____

_____

_____

_____

INDEPENDENCE: The Need For Individuality

If you work alone or strive to be the head of pack, you might be motivated by individuality. If you don't like other people telling you what to do, you are probably highly motivated by individuality.

But individuality is not a high motivator for most people. If it were, there wouldn't be many traditionally employed people in society.

Independent people view themselves as self-sufficient, self-reliant, reliable, and free of the influence of the herd. And they tend to look down on the dependent as weak and unprincipled.

One of the worst insults for the independence motivated person is to be told they are like another person, or that someone else in the group is wearing the same thing they are. They don't want to be like anyone else. They pride themselves in their individualized image, and that they don't follow the crowd. "Everybody's doing it," does not work for them.

By contrast, those not motivated by independence view themselves as devoted, loving, and trusting. They distrust independence as reckless, self-serving, and arrogant. And that's how they view you if you have your own business, consult, or pursue expert status.

Which is to say, they aren't attracted to what you're attracted to. That macho striving actually EWs them. They want someone who will hold them at night, ask their opinion, and work at a stable job no matter how miserable it is.

So while the Marlboro Man was an iconic figure attracting a certain Intended, most people would not be attracted to the extreme independence the figure portrayed. But if you're going to smoke a cigarette at a time when smoking is so tabu, perhaps you look up to someone who can be independent to the point that they don't need a community. They can smoke whenever, and wherever they want.

But people probably aren't passing laws to ban your product or to restrict its use.

If your Intended is independence motivated, you don't want to encourage community, nor rely on testimonials. They will make their decisions based on their own criteria.

EXERCISE: How can you use the independence motivator

to market your company? _____

_____

_____

_____

_____

_____

ORDER: THE NEED FOR ORGANIZED, STABLE, PREDICTABLE ENVIRONMENTS

Order is a prevalent motivator, and is actually hard wired into our psyche. We seek status quo. We fear change. We prize stability. Why? Because change and flux create risk.

Think of the things we say about those seeking adventure, who don't conform to society norms. How do you feel about people who chose not to get jobs in order to pursue their art? What about people who are comfortable not having a physical structure they call home? What about the person who has no illusion that he or she will find "the one," and therefore moves from relationship to relationship?

That said, you are probably not motivated by order. I don't know if you are de-motivated by it, but it would be difficult to be a marketer and prize order. After all, we live in a realm of possibles, maybes, and could-bes. We prize flexibility and spontaneity.

By contrast, most people are at least partially motivated by order. Society prizes people who are neat and tidy. We like people who are in control.

But those motivated by order are difficult to reach. Why? Because they have already created their environments. Any interruption to that environment introduces disorder to their lives, and they work hard to prevent such things.

It is along this line that many Suitors stumble. They tend to not be motivated by order, and yet their intendeds are. The Suitors like to try new things; they are excited by the surprises life offers, and yet, their intendeds don't appreciate roller-coasters.

Again, think of ads that are geared toward the "good life." Is that the life that an ordered person would seek? They want to see pictures of a house well appropriated. A pristine office. A vacation that looks much like their home town.

They don't want the surprise of kiteboarding, dancing in a foreign country, or even a beer that is not a domestic.

If you want an ordered Intended to switch from her current Suitor, you must show her how you are much like her current one, only more stable, neat, and tidy.

EXERCISE: How can you use the order motivator to

market your company? _____

_____

_____

_____

_____

_____

CURIOSITY: THE NEED TO LEARN

This is an interesting motivator. If you are motivated by curiosity, even in the slightest, you don't understand why someone would choose to be ignorant.

And yet wide swathes of the population are not motivated by curiosity. They do not want to learn anything now that they are out of school. They are perfectly content with what they already know. To know more might result in sin or might lead to uncomfortable situations.

Those who are not motivated by curiosity view themselves as sensible and practical. They look at those who are motivated by curiosity as volatile, risky, irresponsible, and flirting with sin.

Of course, the self-described intellectuals believe that they are smart, interesting, engaging, and well, better than the ignorant of society.

If you've bothered to read this far into the book, you are

probably motivated by curiosity. You want to learn more about marketing.

But how many books has your Intended read this year? Statistically, she has probably read fewer than 10 books since the last time she was in school. Of those she has read, very few relate to professional development.

And notice how you feel about someone who is proud that they don't read.

As Suitors we have to carefully check this attitude when we reach out to our Intended. They will be EWed by our Pygmalion attempts. They want to be the way they are, and don't appreciate us shaming them into learning more. Nor do they like how they feel when we reference knowledge, learning, and self improvement.

But those unmotivated by curiosity have other resistances. They are satisfied with the way things are, and they don't have a drive to try something new. If they are already going to Olive Garden every week, it will take a tremendously compelling offer to get them to try your restaurant, or even to order something different on the menu.

If you are motivated by curiosity, it is likely that you don't understand the resistance of your Intended to try something new. You might try something new simply because it is new, while the fact that something is new will keep them from trying it.

So, "new" may not be the best message for most of your Intendeds. They will stay where they are until you give them a compelling reason to try you. And even then, they will feel guilty for not staying in their rut. Things were good the way they were, and now they've disrupted things by trying something new.

They may even get indigestion.

EXERCISE: How can you use the curiosity motivator to market your company? _____

_____

_____

_____

_____

_____

SAVING: THE NEED TO COLLECT

Saving motivated Intendeds are a serious bunch. No jokes, irony, or sarcasm for them. The good news is they need products to save and methods for saving what they already have. If you provide them these means, they will be loyal to you.

Savings motivated Intendeds prize thrift and frugality. They plan ahead by saving more than they need. When they go overboard they appear on *Hoarders*. But for the most part, savers are simply careful, conservative people.

The downside of saving Intendeds, of course, is that they don't spend much money. Most marketers will steer clear of them because of the cost of conversion. It takes a lot of time to get them to buy, in the meantime you need to give them every scrap of information they need to feel comfortable in their decision.

The good news is when they do buy, they are your customer. It will take a long time for them to switch to a competitor. The bad news is it will be a while before they buy again.

In general, unless your product is targeted toward saving, these Intendeds may not be worth too much attention. Be ready, though, for them to find you. Have the information they need available, and when they are looking for you, they'll do the hard work to find you.

Now those not motivated by saving are the fun ones. They love to spend, and they appreciate us giving them the opportunity to spend.

But like any fun woman who may give it up too quickly, she can feel guilty for being easy if we don't assure her after the sale. As long as we show understanding, and don't appear to be taking advantage of her, she'll be fine.

As a Suitor, though, we need to make sure we are fun, engaging, and light-hearted. The Intended not motivated by savings believes she deserves the good things in life. As long as you are the Suitor to provide that, she's yours.

The problem with such vivacious Intendeds is that other Suitors are drawn to her. You'll find a gathering of them following her around. And the more attention she gets, the better she feels. She will flirt with all of them to keep them on the line. You might be one of her admirers, thinking she's going to select you, but you're not much closer than those around you.

You may do better pursuing the saving motivated.

EXERCISE: How can you use the saving motivator to

market your company? _____

_____

_____

_____

_____

_____

HONOR: THE NEED TO BE LOYAL TO THE TRADITIONAL VALUES OF ONE'S CLAN/ETHNIC GROUP

Regardless of your political leanings, your are hard-wired to be loyal to your clan.

In the olden days, it's what propelled people to march on the front lines, knowing that they would be slaughtered by the enemy. But your humbled life would save the king and the kingdom.

Today, there are people who continue to be highly motivated by "traditional values," and by that we mean those values long held by their clan and ethnic group.

Those motivated by traditional values vehemently view non-motivateds as not only wrong, but as a threat to civilization. If your Intended is in this camp, tread carefully, especially if you aren't. But even if you are motivated by your clan or ethnic group's traditional values, it won't matter if your clan or ethnicity is different than theirs.

Of course, honor motivated people do not view themselves as opinionated or bigoted. They see themselves as dutiful, devoted, and dedicated. They use terms like patriotic, loyal, and moral to describe themselves.

Contrarily, those not motivated by honor, believe they are pragmatic, practical, and resourceful. They view those motivated by honor as out of touch, old fashioned, and even bad for society (after all, racism is rooted in honor seekers).

Most marketers and smart Suitors steer clear of this motivator, unless they work for a political party or someone seeking election. In which case, they are closely aligned enough, or pragmatic or devious enough, to work with the honor motivator.

But what if your Intended is motivated by honor, you're not, and your product is attractive to an honor motivated Intended? Well, you're either going to have to convert, or manipulate.

In the end, an honor motivated person believes everyone not in their clan is a threat. As a marketer, it's important that you don't step on the value of your Intended's clan, regardless of the value of your clan, or how you think about its value. When we threaten those values, we threaten their lineage. There isn't much a person won't do to preserve the bloodline.

EXERCISE: How can you use the honor motivator and

traditional values of your Intended's clan to market your company? _____

_____

_____

_____

_____

_____

IDEALISM: THE NEED FOR SOCIAL JUSTICE

On the other side of the spectrum from honor is idealism. Those motivated by idealism look toward the future, instead of back to traditional values. They seek to better the future instead of preserving a past.

But while idealism and honor motivators are often at odds, it is relatively easy for a Suitor to attract an Intended who pursues social justice; after all, what's wrong with social justice?

Sure, in the real world, we might not want to go on a date with a militant vegan, but that doesn't mean we can't market to them. And as long as our product doesn't violate their idealism, we will be fine dodging their protests and activism.

Idealists view themselves as caring, giving, compassionate, and selfless. It is this last quality that the Suitor must step around. If your Intended views herself as selfless, make sure your message doesn't appeal to the ego. Even if the Intended surrounds herself in luxury, she will EW at any attempt to appeal to the part of herself that enjoys such finery.

Like honor motivated people, though, idealists can turn quickly. You might think she has certain passions and concerns, but if you're wrong, you'll lose her. For instance, you might believe that since she protests animal cruelty that she also wants to save the whales. Be careful. She will wonder why you are focussed on whales when dogs are being abused in your own backyard. Or, if she's protesting the deforestation in Brazil, your efforts to plant trees in your home town not only show how uninformed you are, but how you don't understand her.

Unless you speak her language, and are rooted in her sub-culture, walk carefully. Let her tell you what she believes, what she's passionate about. Nod your head, and shut up.

EXERCISE: How can you use the idealism motivator and the need for social justice to market your company?

_____

_____

_____

_____

_____

POWER: THE NEED FOR INFLUENCE OF WILL

Many successful people are motivated by power and the influence of will. For this reason, most advertising and marketing is geared toward power-motivated people.

Those motivated by power are enterprising, aspiring, and ambitious. Better yet, they are influential. This means that if you can attract an Intended who is motivated by power, she will likely tell her friends, and those wanting to be like her will notice that you are her Suitor, and they will take an interest in you.

Of course, her drive to exercise her willpower may keep your Intended away from you. She will not succumb easily to your charm. She may even expect you to swoon before her. After all, she probably understands her value to you. She will expect gifts, and she will expect you to acknowledge her importance to you.

Also, because power motivated people are attractive to companies, your Intended probably has many other Suitors. The competition for her will be intense. Unless you are attractive to her, she probably won't notice you among all the other Suitors. When going after power motivated Intended, make sure you stand taller than everyone else, are better looking than everyone else, and have exactly what she is looking for.

Conversely, the competitive field for those not motivated by power is significantly less. The problem with these people is they are not driven by prominence. They are not proud of their willpower. They are content where they are, so it is difficult to entice them with promises of a better life.

It is also important to realize that Intendeds who are

not motivated by power, view those who are as arrogant, self-centered, and even evil. You are probably motivated by the influence of will at some level; after all, you bought this book to learn new methods for exercising your will. But the more you reveal this characteristic of yours, the more you risk EWing those who are demotivated by power.

Understand that those who are not motivated by power do not view themselves as weak or lazy. Instead, they pride themselves in being humble, simple, even non-ambitious. You can't motivate them to buy from you as long as you devalue their approach to life.

If you are at all motivated by power and the influence of will, it is difficult for you to understand Intendeds who are not like you. You assume that they must find you attractive, must want to improve their station in life, desire to be noticed by others. You don't understand that they pride themselves in being submissive.

Therefore, if you want to attract them, you must check the qualities that you admire, and portray a world that they find attractive. The good news is because of their submissive nature, those not motivated by power will put up with a lot from you, and may even allow you to cajole them into buying something they don't want. Be careful, beneath their humble exterior, resentment will build.

It is always better to be attractive to your Intended instead of pushing them toward a stance that you find attractive.

EXERCISE: How can you use the power motivator and

the need for influence of will to market your company?

_____

_____

_____

_____

_____

VENGEANCE: THE NEED TO STRIKE BACK TO WIN

Yes, it's true, some people have more than a need for power; they've got to be number one. And they're willing to do whatever it takes to win. These are aggressive folks. They are competitive. Just hope they aren't a competitor of yours.

As an Intended, it is important to make sure you help them win. And whatever you do, don't tick them off.

Because of their aggressiveness, those motivated by vengeance are a fickle lot. They may have loyalty for you as long as you're helping them. When they are done with you, or a better Suitor comes along, they have no problem dumping you for them. Try not to take this personally. You've heard of the scorpion asking for a ride on the frog? That's these folks.

A much easier group to attract is those who are not motivated by vengeance. These folks will actually feel sorry for you if you're left in the dust by a vengeance-motivated person. These are kind folks who will forgive your stumbles.

The best way to attract an Intended who is not motivated by vengeance is to be a victim yourself, or at least support causes that fight against aggression and abuse. Those not motivated by vengeance will not pursue their own purposes. Your message cannot be one that they perceive as being self-serving for them. They don't want to feel bribed or flattered. Stick with a social message. Hold their hands and look into their eyes while they discuss all that is wrong with the world.

Like their opposite, Intendeds not motivated by vengeance can also be fickle. If they perceive you aren't sincere, or if they switch causes on you, they will leave you behind.

In general, vengeance-motivated Intendeds are a difficult bunch. Unless your product aligns closely with them, it is better to appeal to other motivators.

EXERCISE: How can you use the vengeance motivator to market your company? _____

_____

_____

_____

_____

_____

Our Intendeds likely have different, sometimes vastly

different, motivators and desires than we do. We may see them as wrong, but they certainly feel we are wrong. As marketers, it is our job to learn their motivators and work with them.

But our tendency is to get them to see the world the way we see it, after all, we are trying to bring them to our point of view. But this doesn't work anymore. Remember, they are in charge, and it our responsibility to be attractive to them. And this begins by working with their motivators.

BE ATTRACTIVE
ON PURPOSE

Peacocking can be fun. It might win you marketing awards. But to be truly attractive, attractive enough to be able to engage our Intended in conversation, we have to be attractive on purpose.

The attraction process begins by first understanding our Intendeds. We need to know the likely personality style of our Debbie Diet Coke, and we need to know what motivates her. Once we know these things, we can present ourselves in a way that is truly attractive to her, not just interesting.

Is she motivated by luxury or security? Does she want loud and flashing, or subtle and quiet? What types of information does she want from us? How does she want to be approached? And how will she make a decision?

We need to know all of these things, and much more, before we can decide what we're going to metaphorically wear tonight.

When an Intended first becomes aware of you, what will she see? What will she remember? Will your collateral attract? Is she motivated to know more about you?

Once you open your mouth and begin talking with your Intended, will she continue to find you attractive?

Finally, if all of this is known, what, ultimately, will motivate her to move forward with you. Does she want you to provide her security or excitement? Status or order?

It takes a lot of work to be a Suitor. There are more considerations than simply a good idea for an ad. Instead of being what you find attractive, or what you think a lot of people might find attractive, you need to focus on your Intended, and make sure you are the only one attractive to her.

And it all has to be done with integrity, because if you do start a relationship with her, she will expect the traits you displayed early in the relationship to still be present.

Good luck.

THE
CONVERSATION
STAGE

THIS IS WHERE IT ALL BEGINS

Looking Good Isn't Enough

Of course, sitting creepily on a bench gawking at beautiful women as they pass doesn't do much for a lonely man. Staring across a bar isn't much more successful. And following an Intended around, hoping she'll approach you could get you arrested.

It doesn't matter how attractive the Suitor is or how long he sits in the right place, the Intended probably won't approach him. That's his job. Remember, in the Courtship Era, consumers are in charge; they expect us to approach them.

In other words, looking pretty is not enough. The Intended has the luxury of sitting coyly on the couch. You, as the Suitor, must approach her and engage her in conversation if you want her business.

There was a time when girls didn't call boys, and they certainly didn't ask boys out on a date.

I'm not suggesting that we should return to that time; what I am saying is that there are certain role expectations in the Courtship Era.

In the old days, it was enough to build a beautiful store, put it in the right place, and put shiny objects in the windows to entice customers to buy.

But malls don't have the same allure today. For a lot less hassle, and perhaps less money, we can get what we need and want online. Sure, it is still fun to shop when we have the time and the interest, but it is an inefficient way to obtain goods.

So, in a sense, we are in an era when the Suitor must not only approach the Intended, but give her a shiny gift to get her email address. Once he has that, he actually has to email her, just like the boys of old had to pick up the phone and risk that first conversation.

Because conversation is where it all begins.

And sometimes where it ends.

How successful you are as a Suitor depends on your approach, and your opener. If you are successful there, you will have a chance to continue in a conversation, and eventually have a chance to be in a relationship with your Intended. Should the opener fail, you will probably not get another opportunity. So the pressure to do it right, and do it well, is intense.

The Suitor's success and failure depends on the conversation stage. Advertising can attract, but conversation is what leads to a relationship.

In the dating realm, this pressure is what we call approach anxiety. There is so much riding on the Suitor's ability to walk up to the Intended and strike up a conversation, that some Suitors stumble, stutter, and say the wrong thing.

While most Intendeds are nice enough to simply smile at lame attempts, the likelihood of experiencing flat-out rejection is immense. Besides the risk, there is also biological pressure to avoid walking up to an Intended and striking up a conversation. Why? Because in the old days, failure to be accepted would result in being ostracized, which would result in a short, difficult life in the wilderness by yourself.

And this is why many marketers find it easier to sit away from their Intended, to not take the risk, to draw pictures and hope she comes over to see what they're creating. Maybe he focusses on sending out tweets, or posting, or buying ad space, but he doesn't take the risk to actively engage her in conversation.

And because of that, he's almost worse than a Caveman. At least the Caveman went after what he wanted instead of hiding behind electronic screens. He understood that just because you build it doesn't mean they will come.

It's A Negative Stage

L et's assume you are attractive to your Intended. You understand what motivates her, you've successfully given her what she wants according to her personality style, you've done everything right.

Now it's time to approach. It's time for your opener.

As soon as you open your mouth, she will be judging you.

The thing to realize about the Conversation Stage is that it is negative. She is looking for reasons you are not the right Suitor for her. You did attract her; you got her attention; now she wants to figure out what's wrong with you.

Think about a time when you found someone attractive from across the room. As you got closer, you noticed some imperfections. Then she opened her mouth and you saw those teeth, or he breathed on you and the odor shoved you backward. And the voice; can you imagine living with that screech day after day?

The initial attraction crumpled under negatives.

But let's say they made it past those initial judgments. Have you ever been attracted to someone until they opened their mouth and began talking to you? Did they say the wrong thing right away? Did they stumble, mumble, and rant in a way that caused you to turn away without giving them the benefit of the doubt? Did a relationship develop later? Or was it dead right then?

This negative analysis continues throughout the Conversation Stage. Maybe you were suave enough to make it through the initial approach, but stumbled later. Many relationships fail further down the road when the Intended finds enough wrong with you to seek another Suitor.

Even if she likes conversing with you, your Intended has other considerations. She has her family to think about. What will it be like introducing this Suitor to her parents? Is this the man she wants to father her children? And will he be a good father? Will he provide? Will he be kind? And so on.

In the Little House on the Prairie days, there was a type of conversation that went on. Someone would walk into a shop and ask the storekeeper for advice on a purchase. Of course the shop owner had biases. Of course he wanted to make a sale. But for the most part, shopkeepers cared enough about their customers to help them through the negative analyzing phase of the conversation.

In the era of the mega-stores, this advice giving was lost. People were hired simply to stock the shelves and run the cash register. If they needed it, they were taught how to sell, but not how to give advice. So people didn't have an ability to analyze whether this purchase was for them, or whether this was a company they wished to do business with.

When they had a bad experience, they had to stand in line at customer service and wait for a bored, but well trained, employee. Eventually, these large stores found it easier to simply take returns than address questions and complaints.

Then the Internet and Web 1.0 made it easier to research a pur- *They are looking for reasons not to buy.* chase before making it. There were forums and places a person could go to discuss a company before engaging it. And when things went badly, they also had a venue to flame their frustrations.

Companies also had a new way to enter into a "conversation" with their prospects. Actually, it was often more like a monologue. For instance, webpages would tout features and benefits. Companies found they could avoid conversations by posting Frequently Asked Questions pages. Besides pop-up messaging services and email, there wasn't an easy way for a prospect to engage a live person in a conversation about a product or service.

With the proliferation of social media, people began to expect a conversation. But of course they rarely got it. It is possible, and relatively inexpensive, to have live people posting and responding to customers in real time. But what do most companies do? They virtually ignore prospects. They treat social media as yet another place to swing their clubs. They don't consider that Intendeds would rather be conversed with than talked to.

To WOO your Intendeds, you need to engage them in conversation, and to realize that in the beginning they will scrutinize you, analyze you, maybe even test you. They will give you resistance with their arms crossed. They aren't sure about you. They want to make sure they can get out of this experience if needed. They want to make sure they make the right decision.

And it's your job to converse with them until they are comfortable with you.

But even when you do strike up a conversation, there are plenty of pitfalls within the conversation. All you have to do is eavesdrop on a few uncomfortable pick-up efforts to understand how badly things can go in a conversation

So while you do need to be in the right place, and it is your responsibility to strike up a conversation. It is even more important to do it well.

FAILURE 1:
WE USE CHEESY,
WORN-OUT LINES

How successful do you think I'll be when I approach a beauty and say, "Heaven must be missing an angel because you're here on earth"?

And yet, how often do we use cheesy, worn-out lines when trying to attract our Intendeds?

"But wait, there's more."

"It slices and dices."

"Buy within in next 30 minutes and receive a free..."

"If I could show you... Would that be valuable to you?"

How special will your Intended feel if you use the same line you use for all the ladies?

It is a natural instinct to use what worked in the past or what's working for your competition, but that will not differentiate you. Worse, she's already heard those lines. You look unoriginal, and she will suspect your intentions.

What happens when we hear the same line over and over? Yes, we tune it out. Think about a billboard you see on your way to work. It registered when it first went up, but then it got irritating, and after a time, you didn't even notice it. Messages become background noise.

That was the problem with banner ads. Way back in the early days of the Web, they worked. Why, because everything was exciting on the new medium. Then banner ads got irritating, and now we don't even notice them. Yes, we're aware of their presence in the periphery of our vision, and they still have an impact, but we really don't notice them. They are like the hundred other souls getting on the plane with us. We have the impression that they are there, but we don't notice them.

Do you know someone who tells the same story over and over again? The second time you heard it, you pretended like it was the first time. The third time, you tried to let them know you'd heard it before. The next time, you gave up. And now you probably avoid the topic or them all together.

Are you like this for your Intended? Are you telling the same story over and over? Giving the same marketing line at every contact? Are they tired of your ads? Are they now avoiding contact with you?

Even the most creative opening line can become tired and worn out after a few uses.

The repetition of your opening lines tells your Intended that she isn't important or valuable enough to have a conversation with. When you use that line on all the ladies, you signal to her that she isn't any more interesting than the crowd. You don't care enough to pay attention to her, to focus on her, to invest time and energy to get to know her.

Remember that Intendeds now expect an original approach that is tailored to them. They also want to have a genuine conversation, not some manufactured experience.

Let's be clear, lines are effective for one-off sales. They still work in infomercials and at carnivals. They aren't WOO because they do not establish a relationship with customers.

That said, when we understand persuasion, we can craft conversation starters and questions that will encourage Intendeds to converse with us. Our lines may sound similar because we are using the same persuasive tools, but our goal should be to make our Intended feel that she is valuable and important, not just another pick-up.

FAILURE 2: WE TALK ABOUT OURSELVES TOO MUCH

Have you ever been stuck at a cocktail party or networking event and the person cornering you talked about themselves for what seemed like hours? There you were, back against the wall, and you couldn't insert a word into the monologue?

Did you say, "Gee, I've enjoyed hearing about you so much, I'd like to have lunch tomorrow to hear more?"

Probably not.

Imagine you are a nervous Suitor, and you just saw the next love of your life. You know you need to strike up a conversation, but you don't know what to say.

What do most people do? Revert to what they know the most about, themselves.

"I do..." "I've done..." "I work for..." "We help people..."

Now, does your Intended find it attractive that all you've done since she met you is brag about yourself? For a time, maybe, if you're funny and entertaining. But after awhile, she'll tire of you talking about you. There will come a time when she will think of you as arrogant.

And yet, what do most companies do? Talk about themselves... All the time.

Look at your webpage. How many times to you use the words "I" or "we"? What's the ratio to the word "you"? Now you might say that's the point of your website, to talk about you. Perhaps.

But now look at your social media posts. What's the ratio of the words I/We to You?

More important, do you only make statements, or do you ask questions?

Why do we go on and on about ourselves? Because we're scared.

We want to control the conversation.

We're like that nervous Suitor, stumbling into a monologue because he doesn't know what else to talk about. If he paused to ask a question, she might not respond. Or if he lets her speak, he can't know what she might say.

If companies let their customers talk, they might hear objections. The customer might tell them what's wrong with them.

But they also might tell the company what they would like.

Conversation is risky, especially since it has an underlying negative analysis, but conversation can also reward us. If we do it correctly.

Failure 3: We Argue with Them

In Caveman days, marketers told us what to think. "This cigarette tastes like a cigarette should." (Really? What exactly should a cigarette taste like? If you could come up with any taste, would you choose this one?). "Because you deserve it." (Do I? And what if I don't want it?) "Must-see TV." (I missed a few programs without deleterious effects.)

In the Courtship Era, telling what they need or want doesn't work. Declaring yourself the king of beers isn't impressive in a democratic market.

Imagine the Suitor approaching an Intended and declaring, "I am exactly what you're looking for in a husband."

She would either snort in derision or slap the fool. If she felt sorry for the man, she might placate with an inquiry as to what led him to believe his preposterous claim. Is there anything he could say at this point that would cause her to change her mind?

Actually there is if she is looking for a quick fling. But that type of Intended won't be there next week. And she won't tell her friends about how great you are.

In any case, an Intended has her own ideas of what she is looking for, and why those qualities are important to her. Telling her she is wrong doesn't work. I mean, have you told a woman she is wrong? How did that work?

Before we approached our Intended, she already had her own Values, Interests, and Priorities (her VIP). These are based on her life to date, how she was raised, her past relationships, and her station in life.

How do we know what her VIPs are? What she's looking for in a Suitor? Or even if she is looking for a Suitor in the first place?

Engage her in conversation.

Salespeople use questions like "What are you looking for in a refrigerator?" Or, "Last time you bought a car, what went into your decision?"

Leading questions like these work for a Caveman because then he can transpose himself into exactly what she is looking for. But if we are Suitors, we must delve a little deeper. After all, if we're lucky, we will be spending a lot of time with the Intended; we might as well know what she's into.

Your Intendeds already have a perception of your company. They believe they understand your market and the positioning of your product. As much as you would like to change their opinions and viewpoints, it isn't worth the effort. Why? Because people will work very hard to maintain the belief that they are correct.

A Suitor who attempts to prove he is right and his Intended is wrong has already lost. Especially if he attempts to use facts to prove his point. She is no longer listening.

And the more he touts the intelligence of his position and supports his rightness, the more barriers she erects.

If it is important to you that your Intendeds understand your position and the value of your products and services, make sure that you focus on those who are already open to your perspective.

For instance, I don't like celery. If you decide I'm your Intended, and you sell celery, you've already lost. You can talk to me all day

> *Customers may or may not be right, but they believe they are. If you want to make the sale, agree with them.*

about the health benefits of celery, note how other people love celery, even remind me that I liked peanut butter and celery as a child; none of it will alter my dislike of celery.

It would be better to pursue someone who likes celery, or who at least is neutral on celery. Then all you have to do is position yourself as their desired source of celery.

Now you probably aren't a purveyor of celery, but perhaps you get the point. Quit chasing after people who don't like you. Don't try to convince them to like what they don't like. There are already plenty of others waiting to be your Intendeds if you only looked their way.

Why is it that we focus on those whom we perceive to be misinformed? Because we have just as much need to be right and validated as they do. Just as you don't want them telling you how bad and wrong you are, they don't want to be told what they want.

Instead, focus on the agreeable. That way, the others will see your popularity, and it will increase your status in their eyes. If you're lucky, they will eventually lower their opinions and be open to your influence. But for now, don't focus on them. Let them go.

Once you find an agreeable prospect, all you need to do at that point is frame your proposition to meet their perspective. Don't try to convince an Intended of something; share with them.

How about this tactic, have them "discover" you, and then have them tell you why you are the best for them. This technique is easier than you think.

The Suitor sees an Intended. He approaches her where she is. He begins by asking her about herself. The Suitor's goal is to learn about her Values, Interests, and Priorities. Once he uncovers these, he can continue to ask her about her opinion on certain qualities he possesses (features and benefits, if you will). If he's careful and creative, she will tell him how she likes his eyes; they are kind (if she likes eyes and prizes kindness). She will tell him how she likes his sense of humor (assuming you have one), and how she is in a hurry to have someone like him in her life (well, she probably wouldn't say it that way, but there are subtle ways to express that priority).

This could not be done in the old days. We didn't have conversations with Intendeds back then. Now, though, we can engage them in dialogue. We can invite them to complete the dreaded survey or engage in their social media presence, either by inviting them into our conversation or responding to their posts and tweets. Done suavely enough, they will eventually tell you how wonderful you are. They will hint that you are the type of person they are looking for.

Failure 4:
We Ask for a Big
Commitment Too
Soon

Have you had this experience? A long lost friend looks you up after all these years. You're excited to reconnect. And when you do, they pitch you a multi-level marketing opportunity. Were you disappointed?

Where many companies totally screw up is they ask for the sale too soon. That worked in high-pressure sales of Caveman days, but not in the Courtship Era.

Let's say I meet a woman for the first time, and we hit it off with a witting and entertaining conversation full of laughs and insights. As the conversation crests, she turns to me and says, "I want you to come to Sunday lunch to meet my parents, and so that my children can meet their future father."

Whoa. And EW.

Or let's go back to the Caveman days of the late 1970s. Mr. Discoman saunters up to a broad and quips, "I'm a man. You're a woman. We both know what we want. So let's get out of here, and go back to my place."

Will that attract your Intended?

EW?

It is best to WOO an Intended through a series of small commitments, and not attempt to seduce her into a big one.

A Caveman must close the deal tonight because he knows if she thinks about it, he'll lose her. She'll understand the folly of the seduction and later feel guilty for going all the way before a date, or loath herself for being so gullible. Later she may blame the Caveman, and she certainly won't talk well of him to other potential customers.

In the Courtship Era, she has the power to warn others. If the Caveman attempts to move to a different neighborhood, or try a different crowd, her words will get there before he does. He can't escape the reputation that she has created for him.

Now she has the power to dominate him over social media platforms. She can make sure that her critique, and words of warning, dominate Google searches, flood Twitter discussions, and generally follow him wherever he goes.

After all, now the Intended is in charge. The Caveman may have won the short game, and been able to play it over and over as he travelled with the carnival, but he has lost his advantage and his ability to prowl.

The Suitor is better suited to WOO. After all, he probably has glowing recommendations from other relationships. Of course, this is one of those places that the analogy falls apart. I mean, in the real world an Intended probably isn't impressed that the Suitor has had many girlfriends, and in fact has many current girlfriends who are all extremely satisfied with his "customer service."

But you get the idea.

In the Courtship Era, a Suitor's reputation supports him and makes him more desirable to an Intended. She has the ability to check references, read testimonials, and even ask others in her network about their experiences.

For that matter, she can ask who would be a better Suitor. This puts greater pressure on a Suitor to protect his reputation, and to not push any Intended into a commitment she is not ready to make.

So a Suitor begins with small commitments, maybe her email address or a Facebook like in exchange for a download.

An invitation for coffee may be in order, where the Suitor demonstrates his generosity and intent by first choosing a safe location for a further discussion, offering to pay a small amount for the privilege. It is there that he can continue the conversation, to learn more about the intended, and share some more about himself.

Small commitments lead to bigger ones. Bigger ones lead to loyalty. And loyalty leads to advocacy.

Think of the metaphorical coffee as a conversation in a Facebook or LinkedIn Group. It's relatively chaperoned, neutral turf, free from the trappings of a sale. It is also where an Intended can feel comfortable learning more about the Suitor, and even draw others into the conversation.

This is why I recommend the use of social media groups. While open groups can be misused by Cavemen who lack social graces, groups are places where Intendeds can freely interact with other Intendeds. Their thoughts and concerns can be aired, expressed, and addressed. And the Suitor, even if it is his group, is either a participant or a moderator.

And yet, even the most disciplined Suitor often falls into Caveman behaviors. Why? Because he has been told from youth to always be closing. He probably even has a book of scripts.

He has quotas. He needs to pay his bills. He doesn't have time for WOO.

But when a Suitor is in a hurry to close the deal, he will not have a customer tomorrow.

It would be better to be patient this evening, ask for a small commitment, and build the relationship.

It's not unlike the old sales funnel, but with a different perspective. Instead of tricking customers into a small sale and then asking for a bigger sale, suckering them into the vortex of the funnel, now the Suitor asks the Intended to coffee, maybe gets her number. Once there, he suggests lunch or maybe an open-air event. There he may suggest a concert, or if he's brave, a movie. Of course a dinner will eventually come. And after several actual dates, he may risk offering to cook for her at his house or hers. And then they are in a tree K I S S I N G.

What are the small commitments you can put into place for your Intended? What are the first, seemingly simple and innocuous, steps you can offer? Don't try to trick her into giving you her email address. Help her genuinely want to give it to you. Don't ask for it so that you can call her in case of an emergency when you know you wouldn't call her in an emergency. Invite her to coffee with an unbidden request for her number or email. If she offers it, thank her for it. Of course, only a fool would leave the scene without giving her your digits, but that is your choice. She may reciprocate, or she may not, either way, you are paying for coffee, hopefully not just your own.

Once you're seated at the coffee shop, don't be the first to touch her. Let her lead. Remember, the Intended is in charge. She is leading you. Don't be in such a rush for a sale that you blow it in the early stages. If she's worth having, she's worth the wait. Also, once she's decided on you, your job gets a lot easier.

WOO through a series of commitments.

Choose three small commitments and list three "next steps" for each one:

_____

_____

_____

_____

_____

_____

_____

_____

_____

Now see if you can list another round of next steps where a request for a sale becomes as natural as inviting her to stay over at your place.

_____

_____

_____

_____

_____

_____

_____

_____

_____

How You Say It Is More Important Than What You Say

Yes, you have a message for your Intended. You are the ideal Suitor for her. She should choose you over all others. And she should get started right away with you.

But she's not ready for your message.

In Caveman days, it didn't matter how receptive customers were to our message; we just kept hitting them over the head until they gave in.

Nowadays, the Suitor must be persuasive. He must be suave. He must have moves like Jagger.

One misplaced word or phrase can destroy his chances, leaving him alone and without customers.

So he must deliver his message in a manner that is persuasive to his Intended. He can attract her with his packaging, but it is his words that will persuade.

Using the work of Robert Cialdini and Kevin Hogan, I have compiled 9 Laws of Persuasion. The reason they are "laws" is because they are hard-wired into our psyche. If you apply these laws correctly, your Intended can't help but be persuaded. It's like a magic pill that compels her to fall in love with you.

The 9 Laws of Persuasion are divided into three categories:

> Internal Psychological Persuaders
>
> Peer Persuaders
>
> Authority Persuaders

It is up to the Suitor which of these categories he'll use. He should definitely begin with the Psychological Persuaders, but can he take advantage of his or other peer relationships to open up his Intended? Does he have the authority to use the last three Laws of Persuasion? Or, more important, does he want to have authority over his Intended? This choice depends on your product and the relationship you are attempting to have with your Intendeds.

Psychological Persuaders

We respond in certain ways simply because we are wired that way. The three Psychological Persuaders are not rational, but they kept us alive in the old days. Of course, I'm not advocating manipulating people with these persuaders, but you should use them when conversing with your Intended.

Law of Scarcity

Could you get a date if you were the last man or woman on the earth?

What if you were the most desirable person, could you strike up a conversation with anyone in the coffee shop?

What if you were the only man or woman in the coffee shop, and you were very desirable, but you could only speak with one other person. Do you think then they would be rushing to get your attention?

Whenever something is in short supply, it becomes more attractive to us. For instance, if you knew there were only 10 copies of this book in existence, and only two of them were available on the open market, the book's value would go up significantly. But since there are as many available as buyers, you believe my hard work and insights are only worth $30 or so. My product is worth less because there is a lot of it.

In your case, this is why your Intendeds are so valuable to you; there are a limited number of them and a lot of Suitors are pursuing them.

So how do you persuade your Intended with scarcity? Let her know your product is in short supply, that you only have so much time to spend with her, that if she can't make a decision now you'll have to work with someone else.

Too often we are so intent on a sale, we spend too much time with an Intended. We let them know they can order whenever they want. We try to be as available as possible.

Now these aren't bad things, but they aren't persuasive.

If a Suitor is always following an Intended around, what is her hurry to act? And let's say he is successfully attractive to her, if she is his only Intended, or worse, if he'll sleep with any Intended, how attractive is he?

But if he will only give her three months to decide on him before he moves to the next Intended, and if he's committed to being with only one woman, does his value go up? Does she have a reason to act?

For instance, a successful suitor approaches a woman by letting her know he only has a few minutes to be with her before catching up with his friends. Now she isn't worried about being stuck with him, having to ask him to leave, or that he'll be hitting on her all night. She'll be more open to his conversation starter. He's let her know that his time is valuable, he has a limited supply to share with her (and that he has friends).

Do your Intendeds know they only have a limited window to work with you? That you won't be bugging her for much longer?

Of course we have developed resistance to other uses of the Law of Scarcity. Isn't it true that we no longer believe people when they tell us there are only four units left, or that it is a limited time offer? This doesn't mean that the Law of Scarcity no longer works; we've simply built up resistance to certain uses of the law.

Because of this law's overuse, we need to apply it in different and in not-so-obvious ways. I am suggesting that in an always-on world, by letting our Intendeds know that we are valuable and that our time and attention are in limited supply, increases our chances of having them listen to us.

In other words, quit spamming her inbox.

The good news is we can show generosity inside the Law of Scarcity.

The reason you over eat at a buffet is because the Law of Scarcity is in play. Before you is more food than you could ever eat, and a cornucopia of contrast. You over eat because while all that food is in front of you here, guess where it isn't? At home

All that food becomes scarce because you can not have access to it once you leave.

EXERCISE: How can you use generosity within the Law of Scarcity? _____

_____

_____

_____

_____

_____

LAW OF CONTRAST

Have you ever been told you look like someone else?

And if you were standing next to that person, would you really look like them?

When Brad Pitt and I are not in the room together, we do have a striking resemblance. But when we are standing next to each other, you realize his imperfections, that he isn't as witty as I am, and his talents are lacking.

The Law of Contrast has traditionally been used with pricing. Normally this book costs $200, but it's yours to-day for $49.95. Sounds like a good deal, right?

Pricing is an art all it's own. Understand that we don't buy rationally. We want a good deal more than we want a good price. When you use the Law of Contrast, you'll be surprised by how much you can charge. Take the most you think people will pay for your product, and make that your "special" price, then double it, and set that as the "regular" price. Today only, they can get your product at 50% off retail. You'll be surprised by your sales.

A more important application of the Law of Contrast, and one that is more in line with WOO Marketing, is the contrast of the price of an item to its value.

In the example above, the one where I stated that this book normally costs $200, did you have some cognitive dissidence? It's because you didn't pay $200. You probably didn't even pay $49.95. Do you know why? Because market expectation for a book is that it costs less than $30. Which is a terrible thing because why would I ever spend the time to write this book, plus all the expenses to produce it for such a low price point? It doesn't make financial sense.

And think of it from your side. Really, what could be the value of information you paid less than $50 for. If I invited you to an intense, three-day training program for $50, wouldn't you be suspicious? How much time and energy do you think I should put into a product that wholesales for less than $15?

But this isn't about me and my book. This is about market expectations and your customers. The market expectation for a book is that it will be ridiculously cheap for the information you receive. Most people feel fine ripping off authors. Why? Because authors have allowed consumers to do this for so long.

If you let your customers undervalue you, they won't respect you.

Important point: people don't buy products, they buy results. Don't sell a product; sell the results.

Did you know that if I didn't sell this information as a book, but as a manual, you would willingly pay much more for it? Why, because you would not be buying a book, but a result.

Market expectation for the product is extremely low, but the value of the information is extremely high. Therefore, if I repackaged this information so that you were buying the value, and not the product, I would be ahead.

For instance, If you applied just one of these Laws of Persuasion, or applied the 16 Motivators to your marketing efforts, and you doubled your sales in three months, what would the information be worth to you? $10,000? What if, using the information you've been given here, you easily increased sales by $100,000 this year, would it be worth $10,000? Of course it would, especially if you could ensure similar increases year after year.

The point is to contrast the value to the price.

What is the value of what you provide to your customers? If you were selling the results, what would the value of those results be to them? How much would they pay to get out of the pain they are currently feeling?

Tell them this value before you give them the price, and they'll understand that they are getting a good deal.

It's the Law of Contrast. The contrast between what they paid and the results they will likely get is large. They are getting a tremendous deal. And who can pass up a good deal?

There are other uses of the Law of Contrast. For instance, if you actually are better than your competition, you should make sure you are standing next to them whenever they appear in front of your Intended. Usually we try to keep our competitors away from our Intended, we don't like her talking about them when we are around.

Have you ever heard women complain about their husbands? Do the men on television and in the movies heighten awareness of their men's shortcomings? What if you were participating in a conversation where someone began complaining about your competitor?

Of course, you don't want to openly brag. Usually a simple expression of surprise that they are being treated so badly suffices. You want them to do the comparison and contrast.

Now let's reverse the Law of Contrast. The further you are away from your competitor, the more similar you look. Are there times when we want to look like a competitor? What if you are distant enough from your Intended that you look like the biggest, best, and most beautiful in your market niche? Would you look similar enough to look like a good deal?

This is an interesting application of the Law of Contrast, but in the Courtship Era, it is rare that we can get this kind of distance from our Intendeds. They want us close, and they want to examine us. Sometimes a closer examination will reveal how we are different from the biggest, best, and most beautiful.

It's usually best to be close to your Intended, and to let her know your value without close comparison to the biggest, best, and most beautiful. After all, she's with you, not with them. You have the advantage.

EXERCISE: Brainstorm ways you can use the Law of Contrast to WOO your Intendeds. _____

_____

_____

_____

_____

_____

LAW OF CONSISTENCY

Of the three laws under the psychology category, the Law of Consistency is the most powerful psychologically. Many studies have explored how strongly we seek consistency.

For instance, if I say you seem the type of person who would attend one of my WOO marketing seminars, and you agree with that assumption, you will act to prove to yourself and me that you are the type of person who will attend. On the other hand, if you told me you are not that type of person, that you already know how to apply the 16 Motivators and the 9 Laws of Persuasion, there is very little I can say that will persuade you differently.

Once people declare something, it is very difficult for them to reverse their declaration. Once a Republican, always a Republican. Once a Democrat, always a Democrat. At least for a few years. People can and do gradually change their minds. But don't count on it with your Intendeds.

Research shows that once we believe something, we will stick to that belief, even when evidence shows that we are wrong. In fact, the more adamantly the information is shared with us, the more deeply rooted we will be in our opinion, no matter how wrong or detrimental it is to us.

For instance, many people believed God would never let man walk on the moon. Well, once we did put a person on the moon, what were those people to say? It was really an elaborate and expensive plot. It was shot on a sound lot in Arizona. And those rock samples from the moon? They aren't real.

It's fascinating research, and fascinating to witness in real life. You've seen the lengths people will go in their conspiracy theories. And the root is simply a belief they had that was shown to be incorrect.

This is why we have to be careful when asking for a commitment too soon. If they say they are not ready to buy, they will never be ready to buy. We need to be careful to not let them reject us, because once they do, they will keep rejecting us. The way they answer our questions will lock them into that opinion.

What if you asked an Intended if she likes you, and she says no? She never will, even if you are the best choice for her.

When it comes to your close, asking her to make a commitment, it is best to always leave yourself wiggle room. Don't ask her for a full commitment.

The warning here is to make sure that when it is time to ask for a commitment that your Intended not state something damaging that you cannot reverse.

Of course you can use the Law of Consistency to your advantage. What if your Intended declares her dissatisfaction with a competitor. She would want to prove to you that she is dissatisfied. If you can get her to say she is looking for a new Suitor, and that she is looking for the qualities you possess, or at least profess, then she will be more likely to choose you.

And once she does, she will want to prove to herself and others that she made a good choice. So have her declare what a good choice she made as often as possible. As long as she isn't second-guessing you, she will be yours.

EXERCISE: List some commitments you could ask of your Intended so she'll remain consistent in her decisions and buy from you. _____

_____

_____

_____

_____

_____

PEER INFLUENCERS

The herd mentality is hard-wired into your psyche. You've had this experience: you're sitting back, relaxing, when suddenly someone nearby jumps or screams, and you jump. And the more nervous they become, the more nervous you become.

Or try this one; you're talking with someone, and they glance suddenly to your left. Where do your eyes shift?

Those around us influence us at a biological level. They jump, we jump. They look, we look. They laugh, we laugh.

When you understand how important peer influence is, you have the opportunity to reach your Intended at a deep level.

LAW OF RAPPORT

If you remember one thing from this book, remember this: "We like that which is like us."

Have you noticed that people look like their dogs? That couples have similar interests and come from similar socio-economic backgrounds? That your friends are a lot like you, and make roughly the same amount of money as you do?

The sooner you become like your Intended, or establish rapport with her, the better things will go for you. Have similar values and insights as she does. Laugh when she does. Even speak the way she does (when was the last time a New Yorker had a good relationship with someone from Alabama)?

As closely as possible (and sometimes this is tricky), you want to mirror your Intended.

For instance, a pick-up technique that has been around forever is to match the breathing rate of the person you are trying to attract. Why does this work? Because you're in sync with her at a physical level. Studies have shown how powerful this technique is.

I know what you're saying, "I can't go around checking out the breathing rate of my customers."

And I'd say, "You're right. I was simply using this as an example of how powerful the Law of Rapport is."

Notice, I started this imaginary conversation with, "I know what you're saying..." Because if you believe I can read your mind, you will also believe we have a lot in common.

Try completing someone else's sentences. Try to get to their conclusion as they do. And they will automatically feel that you get them.

Remember in the Attraction Stage when I said most marketers portray what they find attractive (me in a dress)? Once you understand the power of the Law of Rapport, you will begin to understand why it is important to be attractive to your client. But more important, you will learn how to speak in the language of your Intended. You will begin to adapt to her Values, Interests, and Priorities. You will be Debbie Diet Coke's best friend.

And you will use the word "you" a lot.

If you've been to one of my seminars, you've heard me say that when we speak to everyone, we speak to no one. And you understand the importance of using the word "you" in your copy.

If you haven't yet been, understand that we need to connect with our Intendeds at a deep level, down to where we actually breathe in the same rhythm that they do. Once there, we can begin to anticipate what they are experiencing and feeling. If we tell them what they are probably thinking, they will be more open to us.

Which is to say that Bubba buys from other Bubbas.

Barbie buys from other Barbies.

And you buy from other yous.

EXERCISE: Return to your Debbie Diet Coke. Jot down phrases that you could use to establish rapport with her.

_____

_____

_____

_____

_____

LAW OF RECIPROCITY

This is an important concept: Whoever gives first, gets more.

Do you remember the *Seinfeld* episode where Jerry complains about how the guy took him to the airport, and now he is asking to help him move?

While not universally true, and also not rooted in our biology, when someone gives us something, we feel compelled to return not only the favor, but to return more generously.

While we may be socialized into the Law of Reciprocity, it appears that those of higher status feel even more compelled to give and give well. The thing is, when we give to those who give to us, our return gift is usually worth more than the original gift.

You aren't old enough to remember this reference, but Robert Cialdini demonstrates this law using the Moonies as an example. Before September 11, 2001, we were able to wander airports. The followers of Reverend Sun Myeng Moon approached people in the airport giving them flowers. Once you had a flower in your hand, they would ask for a donation. And most people would give something to the funny looking people.

This strategy was so successful that the Reverend made too much money and went to prison for tax evasion.

Now understand there was no intrinsic value in those flowers. The followers often picked them out of people's yards on the way to the airport. Nor did you want a flower in the first place. And let's say you're getting on a plane, what are you going to do with the flower?

Most people threw them away.

And the Moonie would walk over, pick the flower out of the garbage, and hand it off to someone else.

Yet, even if you received a flower plucked from the garbage, you'd probably still feel compelled to give something in return for the offered flower. Even if you refused, you'd still feel guilty saying no to the Moonie.

Because of the popularity of Caildini's work, companies have been applying this law for decades. Have you been offered SWAG from a company? How about free information from an email or website?

The problem with the overuse of this law is that we've developed a resistance to it. Have you taken SWAG lately without a compulsion to buy from the giver? Have you grabbed free information from someone without a desire to buy from them? And isn't it true that we now expect free stuff?

Well, your intended expects gifts. Other Suitors have given her gifts, and she expects the same from you. And haven't you noticed that the biggest gold-diggers are also the most beautiful women? Why? Because they're used to being given gifts, and now they expect it.

So the first lesson is that the Law of Reciprocity has been so overused, you now have to give gifts to your Intended, she now expects them.

The second lesson is that you will not get the exact return on your investment if she is a desirable Intended.

I don't know who will be reading these words, or where you are in your marketing knowledge. If you are new, I encourage you to understand and apply the Law of Reciprocity. It is an important first step in marketing.

On the other hand, if you've been using this law for some time, let me encourage you to attend one of my sales or marketing workshops. There I teach how sophisticated and successful marketers violate this rule.

Let me tease you with this; Did you know that most successful pick-up artists never buy a woman a drink? Imagine using their technique to gain new clients.

Stepping away from that teaser, understand that I still use the Law of Reciprocity for low-value clients. You've probably seen offers of free information, discounts for programs, and so on.

But when it comes to high-value clients, I don't buy them a drink. They buy me a drink.

EXERCISE: What gifts can you give your Intendeds so that they feel obligated to give back? _____

_____

_____

_____

_____

_____

LAW OF CONFORMITY

Have you noticed that when young people want to rebel, they all dress the same, wear similar make up, and get the same hair cut?

Even in their efforts to establish their independence they conform.

After my college roommate read "The Minister's Black Veil" by Nathaniel Hawthorne, he decided he would express his independence with a Mohawk. Since he did it himself in the mirror, the strip of hair was slightly off center.

The initial ridicule compelled him to totally shave his head, and this was back before a shaved head was stylish. Back then you were either a cancer survivor or a neo-Nazi.

And that's when the ridicule flamed. Some people thought he had cancer. Others laughed at his attempts to establish his independence. His girlfriend broke up with him. I'm sure that today he still shutters at his attempt to not conform.

We have a huge drive to conform with our peer group.

Your Intended will not stray far from her peer group.

Does your organization or your product conform with her peer group? Do they use your product? Similar ones?

Be careful about asking your Intended to leave her friends and family and ride off into the sunset with you. Even if riding into the sunset is what she wants, the pull to conform will keep her the way she is.

You've heard the saying that you are the direct reflection of the five closest people to you. You probably make the same amount as they do, live in a similar neighborhood, and buy similar things.

How many people do you know who are in your field or market niche? How many people do you know who are just like your customers, your Debbie Diet Coke?

To be able to market successfully, we need to be like our Intendeds. More important, we need her friends to like us.

Yes, there are stories about a young lady leaving her family and friends and running off with the sexy man, but the reality is this rarely happens. And even when it does, her tendency is to revert back to where she feels comfortable.

So if we are serious about WOOing our intended we need to join her peer group. Have her friends and family say nice things about us, and we need to conform to her way of doing things. When we do, she will be more likely to move in with us.

EXERCISE: List ways you can conform to your prospects, and identify how buying from you will encourage them to conform to their peer group. _____

_____

_____

_____

_____

_____

AUTHORITY INFLUENCERS

For some of us, it is difficult to conform to our Intendeds's peer group. We have alpha status, so we don't speak their language. It would be difficult for us to establish rapport. And we would rather have them buy us a drink than buy them one.

When we are in this position, we must apply the authority influencers. It is a difficult balancing act to be both a friend and an authority. Whether you use the previous three influencers or the following three will depend on your position in the market, your personality, and your relationship with your Intendeds.

LAW OF POWER

Despite what we think about ourselves, we are all sheep. Some of us bow more easily to authority than others, but the need to follow is hard-wired into our DNA.

Remember the tendency for groups to follow the alpha personality? Because of the desire to follow, it is relatively easy to set yourself as a leader in most groups, unless an alpha has already been established. Usually, you can accomplish alpha status simply by smiling as you walk into a room. (Have you noticed that very few people smile when they enter a room?)

Once you've established your authority in a group, you'll be surprised how powerful the phrases "I need you to..." or "I want you to..." can be.

You'd think that phrases like this would EW Intendeds by sounding commanding or overconfident, but our need to follow keeps most of us from objecting to simple commands.

For instance, there have been several times in the book that I have told you what I wanted you to do, and you probably didn't notice.

Why didn't it come across that I was bossing you around? Because we're socialized to follow. People want to be told what to do even if they are motivated by independence.

So feel comfortable telling your Intended what you want her to do. She will probably feel comfortable following your lead. More important, she'll probably appreciate the guidance.

When we shy away from asking people to act, we create uncertainty in them. They aren't sure what the next step is, or what they are expected to do next. And this unease causes them to seek certainty. And the only way to gain certainty is to withdraw from the situation. In this case, it will mean drawing away from you and your offer.

It would be better to offer guidance and risk resentment. Assuming you are recognized as an authority, you have little to worry about.

EXERCISE: Identify three areas in your sales process where you could say "I need you to..." for instance, "I need you to put your contact information here." _____

_____

_____

_____

_____

_____

Law of Association

Let me ask you a question: Why should I buy the same underwear that Michael Jordan wears?

True, he is an amazing athlete and person, but we don't have the same body size and shape (I know where your mind went just then). So why should I think that something that fits him well should fit me?

Why do people wear jerseys with other people's names on the back? Why is it important that we go to a club where a quasi-celebrity is being paid to make an appearance? Why do we want the signature or picture of people we don't know?

The Law of Association is important to our psyche. I have value because I've met Paris Hilton on several occasions. I've stayed up most of the night with Stan Lee. I eat brunch three stools down from George Maloof. I've met Joe and Katherine Jackson. Kid Rock once sat at my table in a night club, for only a moment, but he did drink some of my vodka.

Am I any more important as a person because I've had these brushes with celebrities?

So why do I feel the need to brag?

We feel better when we associate ourselves with perceived authority.

More important, why was Kim Kardashian paid $50,000 to $70,000 plus travel, plus free booze for her friends, to give two 20 minute appearances at a night club? Because people would stand in line for close to an hour and pay $40 admission to say they had been in the same club as Kim. And it's entirely possible that they left without seeing her.

Do you think you wouldn't fall for such a silly promotion? Do you own a product that a celebrity or perceived authority endorsed? Such as, oh I don't know, a George Foreman Grill?

We think we make rational decisions when we purchase a product that an authority endorsed, but the reality is we rationalize our decision to buy after we get the serotonin release of having bought something an authority also uses.

Put simply, we like to be like Mike.

So think of your Intended. Who does she admire and respect?

If it's you, your job is easy; simply tell her that you use your product.

If it isn't you, who can you align yourself with? What celebrity testimonials can you get.

Sometimes it's not about you, but whom you hang out with.

EXERCISE: If you aren't an authority, how can you use the Law of Association to market your organization, assuming you can't afford an appearance of a Kardashian.

_____

_____

_____

_____

_____

LAW OF EXPECTANCY

Let's assume you are the authority in your Intended's life. You've established yourself as Alpha. You can't pull off the Law of Rapport with her, but you can implement the Law of Expectancy.

Here's what I want you to do. I want you to write down three values you want your Intended to associate with your product. Write them down on the next page:

1. _____

2. _____

3. _____

Did you write something down? Did you tell yourself you would later? Did you want to, but simply skipped ahead to these words?

It's okay if you didn't write anything because I don't care about the assignment. All I wanted to do was prove a point.

I expected you to write three things down, and you wanted to. Whether you did or not depends on your current state and whether or not this is your book.

You and I have a certain relationship. You are reading my words. You may be reading them to discredit me, or because you want to learn something from me. But either way, I'm perceived as enough of an authority to drag you this far into the book.

So when I asked you to write something down, you didn't question my request. Whether you did it or not is irrelevant. You felt like you should.

I don't say this to brag, only to demonstrate that many Suitors shy away from an important law because they feel like they'll EW their Intended, when she will probably do what you ask if you ask with enough authority.

And even if she doesn't comply, she'll want to or feel guilty for not. You simply need to know when to expect and how to word your expectation.

There are subtleties here that require practice, insight, and ethics beyond the scope of these few words, but understand for now that you should not be telling your Intended to "Buy now." What you should be saying is, "I want you to buy now."

The difference between the two statements is immense. When you have established alpha status, and you are the perceived authority, she will listen to your expectations. But if you command her to do something, she'll tell you to buzz off.

The point is the Law of Expectancy is power, but applied incorrectly you'll lose her forever.

EXERCISE: What do you expect your Intendeds to do?

_____

_____

_____

_____

_____

_____

Persuasion Is Only the Beginning

A warning to the persevering Suitor: Persuasion only opens the conversation. It's up to you to keep the conversation going.

Too often Suitors focus on opening lines and fail to remember that openers only give you an excuse to talk. Once an Intended is listening to you, it's up to you to keep the conversation going.

And once it's started, lines won't work.

She wants a genuine discussion. Once you've sparked her interest with an opening line, she wants to know more about you. And remember, the Conversation Stage is a negative stage. She's looking for cracks in your facade. She wants to get at the real you. And she's suspicious that the confidence and compassion you are showing her right now are not real.

Stories may make her say "ahh." Magic tricks may wow her. And jokes may make her laugh. But before she decides to spend more than a few moments with a Suitor, she wants to know the real him.

In the Caveman days, we could hide behind our public image. Our Intendeds never saw behind the veil. But in the Courtship Era, she not only wants to see the real you, she must still like the real you before she gives you her phone number.

This means, young Suitor, that you can learn opening lines, you can apply the 9 Laws of Persuasion, you can use all the tricks, tools, and techniques available, and all you've done is given yourself an audience with her. For the conversation to continue, you must reveal your real self.

Why? Because she now has the ability to find out about the real you whether you tell her or she finds out from someone else.

The curtain between our public personae and the real us is very thin in the Courtship Era. Even the most secretive among us are naked before the world, assuming you have any presence on the Web. If at any time the public and real aspects of our being are not in alignment, our Intendeds will feel that we are trying to deceive them. And once this happens, they will turn to our competitors.

So it is up to us to remain true to ourselves when beginning conversations and applying the 9 Laws of Persuasion. For instance, if you are not an authority, you will be exposed as a fraud. If you use the Law of Rapport and she finds out that you do not speak in her accent and at her tempo, she will feel deceived and turn away from you.

So remain true, and work with what you have and from where you are. Remember, this is a courtship process. Your goal is not a one-night stand. A lot can happen between the initial conversation and the committed relationship. Going for the one-night stand may help you reach the sales numbers for this month, but over time her complaints and negative portrayals of you will hamper future efforts with other Intendeds.

In the social world, everyone will know you are a dog. And once you have that reputation, your choices will be severally limited.

WE DON'T CONTROL THE IMPORTANT CONVERSATIONS

Remember the hapless damsel stuck listening to the over-enthusiastic Caveman talking about himself? We can tell she's miserable, but the Caveman has no idea. He thinks he has control of the conversation. He thinks she's enamored by his successes and exploits. He mistakes her "huh" or "oh my god," for actual interest.

Eventually she slides from under his onslaught, ostensibly to use the restroom.

If you were standing next to the Caveman, he'd turn to you and say, "She digs me," (and he'd use a term like "digs").

He thinks that just because she has been in his presence for this past 11 minutes, and hasn't interrupted him once, and maybe even smiled occasionally, that she has been involved in the conversation.

He doesn't know that she was just passing the time until she could figure out a way to get away.

And once away from the Caveman, the real conversation begins. In the women's restroom. Where the Caveman isn't.

In there, the Intended implores her friend, "Get me out of here. That guy is such a bore. I'm tearing out my fingernails hoping to get away from him."

I want you to remember a time when someone said something bad about you behind your back. Maybe it was untrue. Maybe it was something embarrassing you didn't want people to know.

Do you remember how you felt when you heard about what was said?

Regardless of whether the comment was truthful or embarrassing, the reason you remember it is because you felt out of control. You were unable to control the message.

We are just as out of control when people say good things about us, but we don't remember them because it wasn't embarrassing or hurtful. We appreciate the good messages being spread about us, and we want more of them. But we still don't control what is being said about us in the social media world.

Whether the stories people tell about us are positive or negative, the good news is that people only spread rumors about people they are in a relationship with.

As marketers, we thought we controlled the conversation. We held our monologues through television and print ads, maybe sales calls. But really we weren't conversing with our Intendeds. We were simply listening to our own monologues.

In the typical sales encounter, we were taught to ask leading questions to find the pain. And then, maybe, to intensify the pain. Then solve the pain with our solution. It felt like a conversation because we were asking questions.

But they were our questions. And while the Intended may have played along, they were simply placating us. They weren't invested in the conversation.

The conversation that mattered took place after the ad ended. After we left the sales call. After, to return to the analogy, she went to the restroom with her friend.

That is where and when they are talking about us.

But we don't control or finance these discussions. We are not in their restroom.

And these are the conversations that matter. If she is asking her friend whether she should give us her phone number, we are headed toward a relationship. If she is asking her friend about her opinion of us, we may still have a chance, assuming we haven't EWed her friend.

On the other hand, if she is mocking us, or recounting terri- | *Now we can eaves-* ble things about us, not only have | *drop on what they're* we lost that Intended, but her | *saying about us.* friends as well. And worse, we've lost all the other Intendeds who are paying attention to what the Intended is saying about us.

The advantage that we now have, that Cavemen didn't have, is that we can listen in on these conversations. Sure, we may not be interjecting into the middle of the conversation, but we can listen in to what other Intendeds and our competitors are talking about.

It's as if there were a microphone in the restroom listening to our Intended talking to her friend.

When they are frustrated with us, don't like our interaction, or we EW them out, they have been conditioned to turn to social media and broadcast their experience. Intendeds freely discuss their displeasure across different platforms without thinking that we can and may be listening.

Which is good, and potentially bad.

The reason they are ranting in full view is to maximize the impact of their complaint. That's the bad news. The good news is you (along with everyone else) can see it, and you can respond.

What do Intendeds want? To be compensated for their pain? Maybe. But they really want to be heard. That's why they are airing their displeasure where all can hear them. But more important, they'll appreciate your reaching out to them and taking responsibility.

Think of your response as the chagrined man bringing "I'm sorry" flowers to his wife. He messed up. He knows he messed up. And he's showing he messed up.

You'll find that a simple acknowledgement and an apology will go a long way in short-circuiting their efforts to hurt your reputation. Better yet, they may actually come around. Who knows, you may even make up.

And other Intendeds overhearing the conversation will admire your efforts.

So an important part of your WOOing process should include monitoring what Intendeds say about you, whether in the restroom, over the phone, or on social media. This, of course, is easier if they like you, are connected to you, following you, on whatever platform they are using to communicate with the world.

WOOing involves more than a good pitch, just as a good conversation involves more than good lines. And a gallant

Suitor will have both the comfortable and uncomfortable conversations, and be willing to publicly admit his shortcomings. He will bend a knee and present flowers to show his chagrin.

Just as her complaints with her peers happen where all can read, the Suitor's apology and humble efforts to make amends are also out there for all to see. If performed well and sincerely, he may lose this round, but have a reputation intact when he approaches his next Intended.

It is important to realize that in the Courtship Era, all communication is open for all to see. Not only do we hear the good things people say about us, but the bad are also running rampant across the platforms. And we know that praise only travels so far, but criticism spews into all corners of the social world. It is important that we pursue and preserve all conversations because we aren't simply talking to our Intendeds. Many, many more people are overhearing our conversations, including our competitors.

It Starts Small and Builds

While the Conversation Stage is fraught with mines, ruts, mud, surprise turns, and a myriad of dangers, it is where relationships are built.

It begins with openers. A conversation starter that moves things from an attraction to a relationship.

And while she may have initially found you attractive, and while she may have engaged in the early efforts at conversation, she is constantly looking for signs that something is wrong with you.

Assuming you don't EW her early in the conversation, and assuming she continues to interact with you, you will move into in-depth and revealing discussions. Over time, conversation will deepen in our relationship with our Intended.

Yes, she will be talking about you to her friends and family. But if you've managed the conversation well, the side comments will actually increase her interest in you.

And assuming that all goes well, you will develop a relationship with your Intended. You will be successful in courting her. And you will move through the Conversation Stage into the Relationship stage.

THE
RELATIONSHIP
STAGE

GETTING COMMITMENTS AND CREATING LOYALTY

SMALL LEADS TO BIGGER

An agreement to meet for coffee leads to drinks with friends, leads to a casual dinner, then a more formal dinner and a show, and then a public event together, and eventually, if the Suitor is lucky, he cooks dinner at his house. And if he's really lucky, she stays over.

After months and months, if all goes well, and the Suitor doesn't mess things up too badly along the way, he can keep a toothbrush at her house and she'll claim a few drawers at his place. And then, maybe, they'll move in together.

Congratulations, you now have a committed customer.

And now the fun begins, the real fun.

As a Suitor, your goal is to be more than a one-night stand. The Caveman was satisfied with slam, bam, thank you ma'am. He wanted notches on the bedpost instead of girlfriends. The more women he had in the shortest time, the more he felt like a man.

But in the Courtship Era, this is a short-term strategy. Once word gets out about his morals and intensions, the Caveman will find it difficult to find Intendeds who will fall for his lines. They will have heard about him, and shy away.

He will quickly be out of business.

In the Courtship Era, Suitors must have a long-range plan. They must understand that how they treat this Intended will help or hurt future efforts with other Intendeds. They understand that the point of the Attraction Stage and the Conversation Stage is to lead to the Relationship Stage.

Because the reward is not in the single sale, but in a long-term relationship that is not only mutually satisfying, but in which the Intended will gladly tell about her Suitor to her friends and family.

BECOMING THEIR MY

There is a moment in most relationships when we go from being just another person out there, to their "My."

My girlfriend/boyfriend

My partner

My spouse

Even, my ex

During the Attraction Stage, we are separate from our Intendeds. Through the Conversation Stage we build toward something, though we are still someone they are conversing with. But as we emerge into the Relationship Stage, we go from "There's this guy I'm seeing," to "My date," or maybe, "My boyfriend."

And that's when the relationship has begun.

We are no longer separate from our Intended; we are now an extension of her identity.

We become her My.

In the Courtship Era, this is our goal. We want to move from being a supplier of a product to her My supplier. We want to go from:

A car

A restaurant

A dentist

A counselor

To:

My car

My restaurant

My dentist

My counselor

My [your name here]

Because this is where the magic happens. A whole world of opportunities open up once we become their My.

At the very least, when we are her My, we have beaten our competition. (Yes, they may be her My Ex. Get over it. You won.)

When we are her My, she has made a commitment to us. She will tell her friends about us. We will have more than a third or fourth date. We have a drawer in her bedroom, a toothbrush in her bathroom. And a commitment to be the person she turns to when she needs our products and services.

This is what we used to refer to as brand identity. When we are her My, we have moved from a product on a shelf to a logo she gladly displays to the world. She will travel out of her way to engage with us.

For instance, do you actually use the dry cleaner closest to your house? Is your dentist the one who is most convenient to your office? Do you choose the nearest mechanic? Isn't it true you pass many stores to get to "MY" store?

And all those other businesses you pass probably have similar offerings and similar pricing. Think about the extra time and gas you spend to get to My hair dresser. That is an investment on your part to get to your My.

And now that they are your My, you no longer look at competitors. Unless something happens in the relationship, you will continue to go to your My.

Too often marketers fail to understand the importance of this commitment. In our hurry to attract new customers, and have conversations with those customers, we fail to grasp the importance of moving an Intended past the initial dating stages to the identity stages.

A current customer may be waiting for something better to come along, but committed ones will stay with us longer because they have included us in who they are. We are a part of their life experience. We become part of their definition of self.

> The greatest commitment a customer can give us is to identify with our brand.

To become their My, they need to extend their experience with you. They need to, in essence, go on more than one date with you. And they need to begin making small commitments that involve you.

For instance, I did not have a brand identity with Apple before I bought one. And even then, I don't think Apple was my My until I had purchased more than one of their products (remember the iPod?). But now that I have multiple products, they are my electronic My.

As I write this, I'm hoping my current cell phone can last until the next version of the iPhone comes out because god forbid that I have to buy a new cell phone before Apple offers their latest greatest.

And while it may be true that there are competing cell phones, I won't bother learning about them. I only have eyes for one company. As long as I don't doubt their relationship with me, I will continue to be loyal to them.

Those who have not succumbed to the cult that is Apple may argue that I've overspent on my computer. I'm sure I could have gotten similar technology for a much lower price with someone else, and it doesn't matter to me.

It doesn't matter to a committed Intended if there are other Suitors who are better looking, who have better portfolios, and better opportunities. Once you have become her My Suitor, she will cease to look at other Suitors, or at least she'll be less energetic in her wandering eye.

One Date Doesn't a Relationship Make

Suppose your Intended agrees to a date and that she actually shows up. You do not have a relationship simply because you went on a date. You are not her My yet. You are simply a Suitor she went on a date with.

Yes, it begins with a date, and it is a momentous beginning. But to have a relationship, the first date must lead to many more interactions.

From the example of my relationship with Apple, it is important to note that the first date, the first sale, is only the beginning of a committed relationship.

It is a commitment, yes. But if we stop at the first sale, we've lost out on a great opportunity to become their My.

When I purchased my first iPod, it was good, but other MP3 players were just as good. Yes, they didn't have white headphones, but so what.

My commitment to Apple began with the next purchase, and the next. Now I proudly display their brand wherever I go.

We used to call this a Sales Funnel. Even Cavemen used it. Back then, they'd trick a damsel into making a small commitment, say, to give them her email address or phone number. They did this by offering a trinket in return.

Once they had a way to contact her, they bombarded her with a next level of commitment, say a small sale. Once that sale was made, they up-sold her to something else, and then to something else, until they sucked her into major sales.

And while this Caveman method worked, and still works, Cavemen don't understand what they are seeing, or the potential of the process.

Instead of a Sales Funnel, think of it as a commitment process.

Your Intended agrees to have coffee with you.

Once there, you continue conversing. Learning more about each other. If she's comfortable with how things went, she will agree to make another commitment of time, say a real date. If that goes well, she'll make another commitment of time. And another. And another. And another.

Along the way, you must deliver as promised. You must respect the stage you are in. If a Suitor pushes for too much, too soon, he may get a major sale, but how will she feel in the morning? Is this the basis for a long-term relationship?

In the Courtship Era, it is important that you give your Intendeds many opportunities to commit to you, to make decisions to interact with you, to tell others about their My.

For instance, in the Apple example, I may purchase one product a year from them, if that. My phone and computer last a couple of years. And yet, I have many opportunities to engage with them. They are in conversation with me, and I am friends with other customers and fans.

Apple's competitors go for the single sale. You need a computer? Buy ours. They don't have a long-term strategy for developing a relationship. They are satisfied with this sale, and hope they'll be able to compete when the customer is ready for the next one.

The Suitor seeking a relationship with his Intended realizes that a commitment is more than a date here or there. He becomes her My when she thinks about him even when they are not on a date.

What can you do to stay front-of-mind for your Intended before and after the sale? How can you be a part of her life even when she is not standing in line at the check-out? Can you be in conversation with her when she is not looking and you're not selling?

So lay your funnel down and develop a relationship progression. How will you move your Intended through a series of commitments until you become her My?

EXERCISE: List a series of small commitments you can ask of your Intendeds, several commitments they can make before a sale.

_____

_____

_____

_____

_____

_____

_____

_____

_____

_____

_____

_____

_____

_____

_____

_____

_____

_____

_____

_____

Relationship Mistake #1: It's Not About the Date

Suitors don't understand Intendeds.

You've seen the peacock spreading his wings wide and strutting around squawking. Meanwhile, the peahen goes about her business, not even paying attention to the peacock.

Too often, Suitors do the same thing. In the beginning stages of the relationship they continue their peacocking, not realizing they've already attracted her. Any over preening here irritates her and may come across as showing off, or worse, more concern for looking good than paying attention to the Intended.

In other words, Cavemen focus on impressing her with the restaurant, the wine, and the food they display in front of her. When in fact, she would have much rather a picnic, a walk along the beach, or even a conversation on a park bench.

The fancy dinner makes the Intended look good, but it doesn't necessarily build the relationship. It is the conversation and the time together that deepens the relationship.

Yes, we should strive to provide the best products for your Intended, a luxurious space in which she may shop, and service that excels. These are all attractive things. But if there is no soul behind them, they come across as show.

For instance, have you ever checked into a hotel that had such good customer service it felt fake? You're pretty sure that within all of their repeats of your name that if you told a joke they wouldn't laugh. You'd throw them off their script.

While it's nice to get good service, it isn't a basis for a long-term relationship.

Service is important to the relationship, but relationships aren't based on service. To become their My, we need to move from behind the counter and engage them in conversation, to listen to their concerns, and to interact with them in their lives.

In Caveman days, the woman was the house servant. She became a wife so that she could keep the house clean, cook meals, and crank out brats. In return, the man provided a service by leaving every day to bring home the bacon.

Now we hire people to clean the house, we eat out, and we have fewer children. Furthermore, the woman is just as likely to bring home the bacon, or some of the bacon. More important, the woman doesn't even need a man. And since she's the one we want, we need to do more then to simply provide services.

Any Caveman can service a customer.

Intendeds expect customer service, just as they expect the Suitor to recognize what a privilege it is that the Intended chose him. But this is only the beginning.

While there are levels of customer service, and many Intendeds are drawn to great service, they can get that level of service anywhere. It doesn't necessarily separate one Suitor from another.

The key is to go beyond servicing (wink, wink) your Intended to listening to her, interacting with her, and sharing experiences with her.

Similarly, while she enjoys gifts, a relationship is not based on gifts alone.

And if the relationship is based on gifts, she is a kept woman, not an Intended.

> Whatever we want, we have to be willing to give.

Again, there is a fine line between showing our appreciation with gifts and bribing with gifts. She wants recognition through customer loyalty programs. And she will appreciate gifts that are personalized. But once the gift feels like a bribe to get her to buy something else, she will feel EWed.

It is the thought that counts. Why are you giving the gift? Is it to attract her in the early stages of the relationship? That may work as long as your intention is to intensify the relationship. But as the relationship builds, it is just as important to give simple, meaningful gifts. It might be as simple as a card on her birthday or a thank-you call on the anniversary of doing business with you.

Another problem Suitors need to avoid is only giving gifts when they mess up. It is traditional for a Suitor to give flowers after he has said something incredibly stupid. But if that is the only time he gives gifts, she will associate the gift with unacceptable behavior.

The point is that dates, services, and gifts should be offered in the spirit of deepening your relationship with your Intended. They are meant to intensify your conversations and demonstrate that you recognize and appreciate the business they are doing with you.

If you go over the top, they will become suspicious. If your intentions are Caveman-like, they will get nervous. If they sense that you are only focussed on the sale, or that you give the same gift to all your Intendeds, they will seek a more worthy Suitor.

As you become their My, the cost and flash of dates, gifts, and service become less important than the time spent together and the personalized attention.

For your Intended, it is the thought that counts.

EXERCISE: Think of your customer service program. Identify gifts or outreach that you can offer as "just because" gestures.

_____

_____

_____

_____

_____

_____

_____

_____

_____

_____

_____

_____

_____

_____

_____

_____

_____

_____

_____

_____

_____

WHAT DO THEY SAY ABOUT YOU?

Once you are their My, they want to tell others about their My.

And it is your responsibility to give them stories to tell. What experiences are they having with you? What did you post this week? What did you share with them? How can you make your Intended feel happy to have you as her My, and to share you with her friends?

You've heard of word-of-mouth marketing, guerrilla marketing, and viral marketing. All of these involve people talking about us to their peers and communities. Efforts to artificially create such movements often fail because companies don't understand why their customers would want to spread the word.

Only a Caveman would try to bribe people to talk about them. Bribing only works in the short-term, and others quickly understand that the stories told are not authentic.

A Suitor begins with an authentic relationship. He knows he must first be a My before his Intended will begin to talk about him. Once he is her My, he must then give her stories to share. And if the relationship is deep enough, and the story compelling enough, she will share it with a little bit of prompting from the Suitor.

As long as we are striving to develop our relationships with our customers, they will have more good things to say about us over time. We may drop the ball occasionally, but if we keep playing with them, they will eventually tell about our touchdowns and our wins.

As they speak with their friends, they will naturally mention their My. As they begin to tell stories that include us, our message will spread. Instead of relying on Caveman marketing campaigns, we can let our Intendeds spread the word for us.

Our goal, of course, is that our stories and messages stretch way beyond the reach of our Intendeds, and while this happens occasionally, it is rare. Occasionally, something happens that is so interesting and compelling that people are willing to share it even if they don't have a relationship with the major players of the story.

This story doesn't just need to happen when they visit you, buy from you, or call you. As a Suitor, it is your responsibility to go to them. To engage them where they are. To deliver stories to them.

For instance, you could send them information that they can share with others. Give them a reason to say, "Here is some information that My financial advisor sent me." Post helpful or interesting tidbits they can share. Alert them of events. Be the source of information they can share with others.

As much as we wish it were different, we aren't in control of what messages our customers spread. We can only provide them the experiences that create stories they can share. But since they're the ones spreading the message, they will formulate it in their own words. We have to trust that we did a good enough job framing the experience so that when the message goes out, it's one we appreciate.

I'm sure you've had the experience of someone saying something on your behalf, believing they were doing the right thing, but instead you were embarrassed, or they created problems for you.

Maybe you've been in a relationship where he or she thought they were doing the right thing, but they totally messed things up for you. You were frustrated, but of course you just smiled and told them you love them.

You must have the same attitude. Don't complain about the stories customers tell, or they will feel unappreciated. Thank them, support their efforts, and encourage a conversation with those hearing or reading the story.

Because the one thing we know is that Intendeds talk with each other. They compare their Suitors. They brag, and they complain. A wise Suitor remembers this, and makes sure he doesn't give his Intended any reason to complain.

EXERCISE: What stories are you giving your prospects to share? What information have you shared with them? What could you post or tweet that they could share? List your ideas here.

_____

_____

_____

_____

_____

_____

_____

_____

_____

_____

_____

_____

_____

_____

_____

_____

_____

_____

_____

_____

Does She Wear Your Ring

An often overlooked aspect of the identity part of the relationship is the symbol of the relationship.

Most cultures have a ring or some other adornment that an Intended can wear to display her loyalty to her Suitor. As you become her My, she wants something she can show her friends that displays you. She wants the world to know that you are her Suitor of choice.

And it is up to you to give it to her.

After all, the ring has no meaning if she had to buy it for herself.

Your logo and packaging designs should consider that, as you become her My, she wants something that she can display that tells others about her commitment to you.

Next time you're at a mall, notice how many labels people display. You might be too practical to shop labels, or too snobby to buy from designers who stitch their labels where all can see them, but understand that your Intendeds display labels. Why? Because they want others to know what products and companies they have relationships with.

Does the shirt feel different when it has a polo rider on it, an alligator, or a penguin? Same shirt, right? Different feel.

The difference is the logo.

Logo and packaging design isn't about being attractive or making a statement, but giving Intendeds something they can identify with. Their Coach bag is My bag. Their car is My Benz.

The more committed your Intended is to you, the more she wants to display that commitment. She wants the world to know she has a My, and she wants to be affirmed by her My.

But most companies are egotistical about their logo. They don't create something that inspires a relationship. Instead, they use the logo as an opportunity to "brand" their customers. And people, in general, do not like to be branded.

For instance, the Dell logo does not feel friendly. It is, however, a testament to Michael Dell's business model. Do you have a relationship with Michael Dell? What about his computers?

But the Apple logo has an aesthetic. Better yet, the design of their products has a certain feel. My MacBook Pro looks different from other laptops, even though I've covered the Apple logo with my own branding skin. When I pull out my laptop in an airport bar, people recognize my computer and my My.

The guy down the bar with his HP doesn't have the same feeling about his electronic choice. Nor do people notice his computer.

Even if we are both frustrated with our computers, or are ready to upgrade, I will reinvest with my My, but he may try a different brand of PC. Maybe, he may even join me as a fanatic of Apple.

The point is that when it comes to logo and product design, you want to give your Intendeds something they can attach a feeling to. How does Louis Vuitton feel? What about a Volvo? Does H&R Block have a feeling? How about Progressive Insurance?

If all dentists feel the same, what can you do with your logo and the design of the experience you offer to encourage people to identify with you? And once they identify with you, you also want to make it easy to share their experience with others.

The point is if your Intendeds will be displaying your products where others can see them, carefully design your logo and product design to allow them to place a feeling on your products. If, however, you provide your Intendeds with less tangible services, give them stories they can share with others.

In either case, it is not about you, but about your Intendeds. They want to tell others about their My. You simply need to provide them with material to share, and the visual trappings that allow others to admire their relationship, ask questions, or simply nod in recognition.

EXERCISE: Brainstorm ways you can give your prospects symbols of the relationship that they can share and display.

_____

_____

_____

_____

_____

_____

_____

_____

_____

_____

_____

_____

_____

_____

_____

_____

_____

_____

_____

_____

_____

Relationship Mistake #2: Taking Them For Granted

If you've ever been in a long-term relationship that failed, you can probably point to a time when you began to take each other for granted.

Our lives get into a routine. We do the same-old-same-old. We let ourselves go. And we sit on the couch every evening watching the television.

The romance is gone.

And soon our partner may be gone as well.

Business isn't much different. We work hard to get them, but once we have them, we begin to take them for granted. They become yesterday's news. They feel unappreciated.

Worse, as we begin to take them for granted, we let ourselves go when we are around them. We no longer strive to be attractive to them because we feel we have them. And as we let ourselves go, they begin to feel we deceived them by displaying an image of what we are not.

Eventually, they will not want to be around us. They will look elsewhere, noticing how attractive other Suitors are. They will hear how other Suitors continue to fawn over their Intendeds, and they will want to be treated this way. And then there will come a time when she is no longer there for us.

Taking them for granted is easy, but it becomes very expensive. When they leave us, divorce us, it ends up costing us a lot of money.

And attracting their replacements isn't cheap either.

In real life, if you're in a long-term relationship, you probably don't realize how expensive dating is, especially for those who are in a competitive market. And I'm not just talking about the cost of dinners and a movie, because hopefully you still enjoy those with your current relationship.

It takes a lot of time and effort to attract a new Intended. It's much easier, and thus less expensive in time, effort, and investment, to keep the one you have.

And not just keep her, but deepen your relationship with her every day, so that the rewards you receive from the relationship increase and enhance.

Wouldn't it be better to keep the customers we already have? You've invested a lot to get them, and there isn't much cost in keeping them. Better yet, once you are their My, they will tell others about you, and you will have more business and a relatively low cost of outreach.

But even if we know it is less effort and less cost to keep our current Intendeds, our tendency is to take them for granted. We feel that just because they've bought from us before, or just because they've been loyal, everything will remain the same.

And it never does.

Customers have a whole lot less invested in the relationship than we do. It is easier for them to walk than for us to see them go.

And because of this, it is up to us to keep the relationship alive, to keep their eyes from a wondering toward a better Suitor.

Because if they've been with you for a while, and they feel compelled to leave, they must be upset with you. In their effort to justify to their friends why their decision was not a good one, they will make sure you are the villain of their story. There is no way you will look good, or that they won't spread the word about how poorly they were treated.

> Commitments are more than a single event. They are continuous.

Worse, her friends and followers will hear about how much better her new Suitor is. Word will spread quickly about how you blew it, and how wonderful your competitors are, leaving you with a double loss.

So it makes sense for us to continue to build relationships with our current customers. And this is done through continuing to be attractive to them and continuing to engage them in conversation.

You know those people who let themselves go after they get married. That guy sitting in the Lazyboy with his gut expanding every year, his hair woefully out of style, and he hasn't bothered to buy new clothes for some time.

Is he still attractive to his wife? Maybe, if she finds his sloth endearing. More likely, she loses her attraction to him. She may stay in the relationship out of loyalty, but will probably cease to invest in the relationship. Or to put it crudely, she's less likely to put out.

Isn't it true that when we were first WOOing our Intended we exercised, watched what we ate, and made sure our clothes were washed?

Are we still doing those things? Do we still look good to her? What is it that they found attractive about us in the beginning? What do they find attractive now? Do we measure up to their standards of attractiveness?

The problem is most marketing campaigns only focus on being attractive to new Intendeds, not to the customers we already have. We only work to get through the acquisition stage, and then forget to stay attractive. Once Intendeds are clients, the campaign ceases. And they feel taken for granted.

Isn't it also true that relationships only build over time when both parties talk with each other?

Let's assume we aren't the slovenly man on his Lazyboy chair watching hours of televised sports, not interacting with our Intendeds. Instead, isn't it true, that we are more like the workaholic husband who is never home?

We are focused on business. Attracting and conversing with new Intendeds. Running and expanding our businesses. While we are at work, we occasionally think about the Intendeds we already have, but our focus is not on them.

They are alone, at home, with nothing more to do other than talk with their friends about their frustrations with their relationship. They will hear what wonderful things other Suitors are doing with their Intendeds. And their friends will give them advice about how they should leave you for someone who treats them like a treasure.

And then, maybe another Suitor will charm with how much better he meets her needs and wants. He will listen to her complaints, ask questions, make her laugh, and generally engage her in the conversations she's not having at home.

If we care about our current relationships, we will continue to engage them in conversations. We will sit down and ask them about their concerns and interests. We will share with them our considerations. They will feel a part of our daily lives.

In other words, every WOO Marketing campaign must involve engaging current customers in conversations. We must ask questions about their experiences, listen when they tell us how we can improve, and share with them what is important to our company.

You need to give her something she can tell her friends about how wonderful you are. When she's bragging about you, your competitors will not have an opportunity to crack your relationship. And over time, your relationship will intensify.

Loyalty programs begin with being loyal to them. By focusing on your customers, you encourage their loyalty.

EXERCISE: What can you do to continue to engage your customers? What steps can you take to engage them in conversations with you, and about you?

_____

_____

_____

_____

_____

_____

_____

_____

_____

_____

_____

_____

_____

_____

_____

_____

_____

_____

_____

Let them Give Back

Any relationship, by definition, involves giving and taking by both parties. How long would you be friends with someone who always let you pick up the check?

Or how long would a Suitor pursue and Intended who didn't give something in return for the trinkets, dinners, dancing, and attention?

A thief, by definition, is someone who takes and doesn't give. Even a gold-digger gives up something for the gold.

For a relationship with your Intendeds to become and remain strong, they must have the opportunity to give back. Better yet, when we are their My, they want to give back. They want to help us expand and succeed. After all, we are a reflection of them and their choices.

So give them the opportunity to give back to the relationship. And not just with their money. Paying money for a good or service is a commitment, but only in comparison to how much money they still have, how much they spend on other things, and for as long as the money is missed.

In other words, simply buying something is a short-term commitment. Soon the lost money will be replaced.

If our goal is to have loyal and repeat customers, we will encourage more than a simple transaction of money for a product; we will ask them to express their commitment to us, whether that be by sharing their experience with others, commenting on or contributing to our marketing efforts, or simply joining a community of other loyal customers.

Social media, of course, offers many opportunities for extending the customer relationship beyond the first transaction.

Could your company benefit from a closer conversation with your Intendeds? Is it possible that their insights as customers would give you a better perspective on customer service or product design?

It's important to realize that Intendeds won't volunteer to work with you. You have to ask them to participate. For instance, when was the last time you volunteered a recommendation? Searched for and joined a Facebook group? Isn't it true you were asked to act before you gave to a charity?

So ask, but in a way that is appealing to your customers. Don't ask for too much too soon. You don't want to EW customers by asking them to spread the word on your behalf if they are still evaluating whether or not they want to have you as their My.

The principle of progressive commitments applies. Maybe you begin with a survey soliciting their comments about their experience. Then you could ask them for a testimonial. Later, ask them for a social media mention. Still later they could share their experiences with a prospect, and so on.

The temptation here is to be self-serving. As you formulate ideas for engaging your customers and encouraging them to give back, don't just focus on how they can further benefit you. You then become a taker. Consider that strong relationships exist when the parties work toward a common goal.

What if your Intendeds partnered with you on a community or charitable effort? What if, while helping others, they agreed to join your team, maybe even wear your T-shirt while doing so.

The more contact your Intendeds have with you after the sale, the more loyal they'll be. They will also be more likely to tell others about their My. And the more good you can accomplish by extending the influence of your network of customers.

And best of all, other Intendeds are more likely to notice and find you an attractive Suitor. It's a great "have your cake and eat it" situation. While solidifying your relationship with your current Intendeds, you attract new Intendeds, and do some good in the process. Besides the loss of effort and a shift in focus, there isn't a downside of asking your Intendeds to give back to the relationship.

EXERCISE: List ideas for engaging your current customers. How can they give to the relationship?

_____

_____

_____

_____

_____

_____

_____

_____

_____

_____

_____

_____

_____

_____

_____

_____

_____

_____

_____

_____

_____

_____

It's about the Relationship

In the Caveman days, it was about the single sale. Sometimes, if competition and pricing were right, Cavemen would get repeat business.

But now that they are in charge, our focus must be on the relationship. After all, it is easier to develop the relationship you have than to attract and converse through a series of small commitments to a new one, as any man or woman enjoying a movie on the livingroom couch with their spouse knows.

So while it is important to expand our customer base, finding new prospects and converting them into customers, let's not forget the ones we have.

In other words, let's put service back into customer service. And converse, truly converse, with them. And make it easy for our customers to remain loyal as they tell others about what a wonderful company we are.

THE EULOGY

R.I.P.

REST IN PEACE CAVEMAN

Ladies and Gentleman, raise your glasses in honor of the Caveman's passing. Let's acknowledge his contribution, the lessons he taught us, and toast to the future that now lies ahead of us.

It's nothing personal against the Caveman. Before technology, few things worked better than the club. And people responded to the club. It was effective. And large companies, whole industries, and even the media were built by some powerful and notable Cavemen.

Take a trip to the grocery store and notice all those items on the shelves, notice that most of them come from a few major companies. Could such conglomerates have been built without some serious club swinging?

Could technologies like radio, television, and the Web exist without interruptions?

What about the sore heads that paved the way for the very technologies that ushered in the Courtship Era? Have you heard the stories of the great leaders that put that phone in your hands or tablet on your lap?

It's just that things work until they don't.

And when they don't, it's good to say good-bye, acknowledge the accomplishments, be thankful for the lessons learned, and raise a drink to toast the past and the future. So clink your glasses again.

Why is it important to say goodbye to the Caveman? Because most of us learned from the great Cavemen of previous generations.

Who taught you how to acquire customers? Who taught you how to treat them once you had them? Sure a few leaders have emerged in the last few years to cry a different message from the wilderness, but they've gotten recognition because they are different.

What seems natural is what we've always done. Change is difficult, especially when decades of success have come from Caveman tactics. The brain's natural tendency in the face of new environments and technology is to continue what we've always done.

Especially if we're older.

Especially if we can remember the good old Caveman days.

So we have a choice, we can be old farts talking about how things used to be and complaining about all the new-fangled technology and the kids these days. Or we can adapt.

And just as the real cavemen receded with the Agricultural Era, companies that don't adapt to the new market realities and customer expectations will get an evolutionary shove out of the market.

It's up to us to acknowledge what the Caveman Era accomplished, and what the legendary Cavemen taught us, and then turn toward the new future.

After all, our prospects and customers are in the present and in the future. They are glad to be free from their the past. They like the market power they now have. And they demand different from the companies vying for their money.

If our survival depends on our adaptation, the one smart thing to do is leave Caveman ways in the past and begin to WOO customers.

Goodbye Caveman. We will miss you.

And now to you, Dear Reader... I don't know if the analogy of the Suitor and his Intended worked for you. I certainly hope it didn't distract from some of the ideas and principles I've shared here. At the very least, I hope that you realize that the market has changed, and that it is up to us to adapt to new realities and relationships.

Also, as creepy as this may be for you, I consider you My Intended. I wish to extend and deepen my relationship with you. Please connect with me on social media. Feel free to email me (jp@JonathanPetersPhD.com). Let's converse.

For now, raise your glass once again, and toast to us.

ONCE UPON A TIME...

A YOUNG MAN FELL IN LOVE AT FIRST SIGHT.

BUT HE WAS SMART ENOUGH TO KNOW THAT MANY OTHERS WOULD BE VYING FOR HER ATTENTION.

SO HE DRESSED TO IMPRESS, AND WASN'T ASHAMED TO GO THE MOVIES WHERE SHE WAS, THE CHARITIES SHE SUPPORTED, AND THE CHICK WINE TASTINGS. BECAUSE HE KNEW HE NEEDED TO BE WHERE SHE WAS.

HE ENGAGED HER IN CONVERSATION, ASKING QUESTIONS, AND GENUINELY LISTENING.

AND THEN HE ASKED HER TO COFFEE. AND THEN TO LUNCH. AND THEN TO DINNER.

NOW SHE'S HIS.

BETTER YET, SHE'S TELLING OTHERS HOW WONDERFUL HE IS.

AND ALL HE HAD TO DO WAS WOO HER.

ABOUT
JONATHAN PETERS, PHD

Jonathan Peters, PhD asks the question, "What is persuasive," and he shares what he discovers.

As an international speaker Jonathan understands that best way to learn is to laugh. He has entertained audiences from Melbourne, Australia to Augusta, Maine, teaching them cutting-edge principles and methods. Audiences leave his events ready for change.

As a trainer, Jonathan works with organizations to craft their marketing messages, he also equips them to succeed in the months and years ahead.

As a writer, Jonathan has been involved in numerous marketing campaigns. More interestingly, he has ghost-written close to 30 books besides his own.

Jonathan also maintains his academic credentials at the University of Nevada, Las Vegas, where he prepares future business leaders for the real world.

But his best accolade is the full and exciting life he lives.

The fun continues...

This book is only part of the **Caveman Trilogy**. You've begun with attracting and keeping clients. After our Intendeds choose us, then what?

Cavemen Don't Get Customer Service: Improving Customer Experience and Loyalty.

You've attracted, communicated, and lead your customers through a series of commitments, now you are their MY. How do we apply the principles of WOO Marketing to customers servives? In other words, it's one thing to get a date, it's quite another build a successful lifetime relationship.

Cavemen Can't Lead: Leadership for Organizational Success in the Social Era

There comes a time when others must interact with your customers. How will you lead the WOO Troops? Just as you must consider the 16 Motivators when attracting and keeping customers, you also must use them to attract and keep the best employees. You can't do it all yourself, so why not have the best and keep the best?

THE 16 MOTIVATORS MARKETING COURSE

The course includes:

The Assessment: Yes, we first need to understand us before we can communicate with them. But the real reason for taking the assessment is to begin thinking about how your clients might answer differently.

Debbie Diet Coke Exercise: This one-hour recorded webinar walks you through the process of creating your customer personae.

The 16 Motivators audio program: Learn how they make decision. Quiet killing the sale before it starts. Instead, understand their motivators and how to work with them.

Plus.... **Full Scholarship** in the
Online Introductory Copywriting Course
This multi-week course applies all that you've learned to communication strategies with prospective and current customers.

You've enjoyed reading his insights . . .

Now, bring Jonathan to speak to your organization or at your event.

Jonathan Peters, PhD is a highly sought after speaker and trainer. His emphasis is always on fun and learning as he delivers high-energy, high-content keynotes and training, along with applications to lead in the market and in the real world

Jonathan's passion is persuasive communication. He helps organizations acquire and retain their customers.

He also works with leaders to motivate their teams using the latest techniques and information about what moves people to action.

He is a natural motivator, optimist and entertainer. His presentations are inspirational, funny, and focused on helping you achieve results.

You can research more about Jonathan by visiting his website JonathanPetersPhD.com.

Here you'll find his blog, speaking calendar, and different resources he has available; you can even sign up for his newsletter.

Or you can simply email him at...

jp@JonathanPetersPhD.com

Go ahead, break the rules, and tear out this page.